REGGAE ISLAND

REGGAE ISLAND

Jamaican Music in the Digital Age

Brian Jahn
Tom Weber

DA CAPO PRESS • NEW YORK

Library of Congress Cataloging-in-Publication Data

Reggae island: Jamaican music in the digital age / Brian Jahn [photographs];
 [text edited by] Tom Weber.—1st Da Capo Press ed.; rev. and expanded.
     p.   cm.
 Originally published: Jamaica: Kingston Publishers, 1992.
 ISBN 0-306-80853-6 (alk. paper)
 1. Reggae musicians—Jamaica—Interviews. 2. Reggae music—Jamaica—History and criticism. I. Jahn, Brian. II. Weber, Tom.
ML3532.R45 1998
781.646′097292—dc21   98-8655
                                                                              CIP
                                                                              MN

First Da Capo Press edition 1998

Published by Da Capo Press, Inc.
A Subsidiary of Plenum Publishing Corporation
233 Spring Street, New York, N.Y. 10013

Manufactured in the United States of America

Dedicated
to the people of
JAMAICA
both at home
and abroad

Contents

Introduction

You know what I think? I think that you're going to discover something very important about all these interviews that you're getting. Is that there's one common thing about all of them, whatever that is. Because all of the different reggae artists, producers, and all of that is like the members of the body, like the hand do a different work, and the feet do a different work, and the eyes and the ears, but they're all connected to the same body. So you're going to find one common thing. Everyone might put their word across different, but I'm telling you now, look for that common thing, that will be there. Most of us will know where the talent come from, how we should exercise it, how to be exposed, what kind of channel we have to take. Most of us have this common misfortune vibe at the initial stage of the career, and have to apply a specific method to go through, like determination and all the other laws of success. I won't mention any more, man, you going to discover it. I don't want you to know it from now, 'cause if you know it from now, you won't discover it for yourselves.

—Tony Rebel

The dance hall is not so much a place as a state of mind, a spontaneous happening that occurs when hundreds of people get together in a building or yard or field or parking lot and tap into thousands of watts of raw reggae power, crisp treble, strong midrange, and a low end so potent that it feels like an earthquake. People are dancing, some with partners, but most of them facing the stage and mammoth speaker stacks that are the energy source. There is no live band, only records (for this is the way it started).

The selecter plays the turntables like a virtuoso, teasing the crowd, picking up the needle midway through a tune, hesitating for a second, and then playing it again from the start. The dance hall is built on a groove, and he keeps the groove going all night, working the crowd into a frenzy and then letting them cool down. He plays instrumental rhythm tracks—riddims—off the "B" sides of countless seven-inch 45s as a parade of singers and DJs deconstruct the hit songs and rebuild them in radically different ways. Some talk about love and others about guns, some about expensive cars and others about food prices, but they are talking to the people through this powerful medium, and the people are talking back to them.

Competition is fierce, and the crowd is demanding, but a performer who really gets the people moving is cheered long and hard. Some of the oldest traditions in reggae—the recycling of popular riddims, the stop-and-start, "wheel and come again" style of presentation—have their origins here. Once, this scene was confined to Jamaica; today, it could be happening anywhere on the planet.

The Jamaican dance hall is and always has been the heart and soul of reggae music: it is nightclub, news medium, gathering place, church, theater, and schoolhouse all rolled into one. For the hundreds and hundreds of aspiring artists who gravitate from country to city in a never-ending stream, the dance hall is a creative outlet and gateway to fame and glory. We like to use the term the way Bunny Wailer does, as a metaphor for the enduring spirit of the Jamaican people expressed in music.

In the past ten years, "dancehall" has come to have another meaning, the contemporary style of up-tempo reggae, chatted or sung over computerized rhythm tracks. There is no question that dancehall is the dominant style of the day; the dancehall sound is so popular that dozens of older artists have broken with tradition and made dancehall records. There is also no doubt that the dancehall phenomenon has sparked more worldwide interest in Jamaican music than anything in a long time. A family reunion of sorts has taken place between reggae and rap: each has influenced the other, and reggae has penetrated the vast North American urban audience for the first time. For a while, there was a rush by the major record labels to sign dancehall artists, but now the inevitable shake-out is taking place and the "majors" are losing interest again.

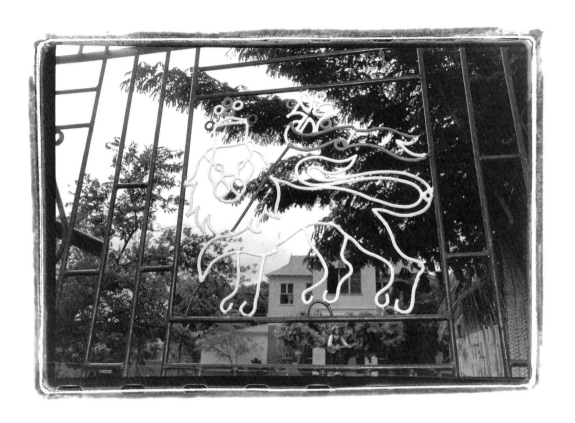

Ask any of the old-timers around the music business, in Kingston or abroad, and they'll tell you that all of this has happened before; the same boom-or-bust cycle has accompanied each of the major stylistic phases in reggae: ska and rock steady in the Sixties, roots reggae in the Seventies, rockers in the Eighties, dancehall today. The styles may change, but the music is never-ending. The veterans—singers, musicians, DJs, producers—have endured through all these phases by doing the steady work that keeps reggae alive: pumping out records for radio, juke box, and dance hall; going on tour; trying to make the people move. In few other forms of popular music do you find people like Alton Ellis and Ken Boothe, with hit records going back almost forty years, still putting out new songs side-by-side with the latest teenage DJ sensation, or groups like Culture and Burning Spear, touring Europe, Africa, and Asia year-in and year-out, spreading the reggae vibe around the globe. All of this is rooted in the dance hall, which is to say the spirit of the Jamaican people expressed in music.

Reggae is like a hardy plant that grows naturally in Jamaican soil, but lends itself easily to transplantation. Perhaps this is because reggae itself is a combination of many influences, from *Pocomania* rhythms to American rhythm and blues, from European nursery rhymes to African trickster stories, from Niyabinghi drums to digital samplers. Perhaps it is because reggae's message of spirituality, peace, love, and understanding finds a lot of resonance in this troubled world. Perhaps it is because people everywhere love to dance. For all of these reasons and more, reggae has taken root in distant countries and has changed and envigorated itself in the process; it remains strong at the core because it is deeply rooted among the people.

In Kenya, where reggae is officially banned from the state-run radio for its political content, the *metatu* buses—equipped with powerful sound systems—serve as mobile discos; young people ride them all day to hear the newest reggae tunes and want to grow up to be bus drivers. In Nigeria a group called the Mandators plays roots reggae with a west African accent. In Japan crowds of 60,000 or more are common at reggae concerts, and nightclubs compete to be the first to play the newest hit singles from the Kingston studios. In Panama, Puerto Rico, and Mexico, artists like El General and La Atrevida (Rude Girl) put out reggae records with a Latin flavor. In the southwestern United States, an isolated Native American tribe called the Havasupai—who battled the government over land rights in the Eighties and are now threatened by uranium mining—are ardent reg-

gae fans; in its message about struggle and oppression, they believe reggae tells their story.

It seems a long time since the sunny February afternoon in 1992 when Tony Rebel predicted, somewhat playfully, that we'd find one common thread connecting all the interviews that follow. There have been many changes since this project started, some happy (reggae seems stronger than ever) and some sad (the premature deaths of promising young artists Panhead and Garnett Silk). Many interviews and photo sessions later, we think we've found the common thread, and we hope that you will find it, too. Like Rebel, we aren't going to tell you, or you won't discover it for yourselves.

We went to Jamaica, the wellspring of a music that has captivated the world, with our heads full of questions. Why do people all over the world—Asians, Africans, Arabs, Europeans, North and South Americans—connect with reggae music, even though they don't share a common culture and may not understand the words? Why do you find the same reggae rhythms being played everywhere on the globe? How has reggae changed since the passing of Bob Marley, who first brought this Kingston ghetto music to the worldwide arena, and where is reggae headed? What do the people think about all of this on the streets of Kingston, in the studios, and in the dance halls where it all started sometime back in the Fifties? Have the roots been lost, as Burning Spear claims, or are they alive?

In this book the artists and producers who make reggae music speak for themselves. Interviews were transcribed faithfully and edited only for length, although Standard English spelling was used for the sake of readability. No disrespect is intended to those who are left out, since this book is not intended as a comprehensive "Who's Who" of reggae. What you see in these pages are the faces, the surroundings, and the spoken words of the people who have taken this island music from the dance halls of Reggae Jamaica to the farthest corners of the world.

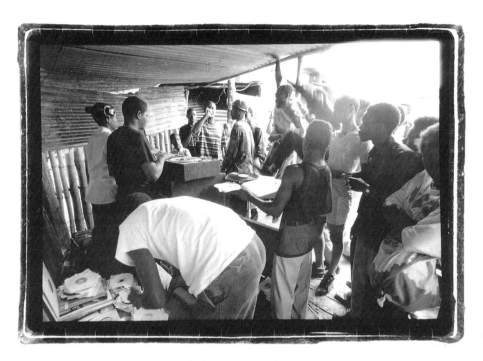

COUNTRY SESSION

KINGSTON SESSION

JUNIOR REID LIVE AT THE UNIVERSITY OF WEST INDIES

Dancehall Version

Rasta consciousness has returned to dancehall music, or so we hear.

Ever since the explosion in dancehall-style reggae in the late Eighties, many of the leading DJs have been dogged by criticism: for macho posturing; for degrading women; for cultivating materialistic values; for glorifying drugs, crime, violence, and automatic weapons. For a time in the early Nineties, you could hardly open a *Daily Gleaner* without reading about the harmful effects of DJ music on Jamaican youth, usually written by a clergyman or other establishment type. About the same time, many of the same things were being said about American rap—as they have been said about practically any form of music that becomes hugely popular among young people: rock and roll, calypso, blues, jazz, juju, and "township jive," to name just a few. What the establishment types always seem to be saying is: "These musicians are speaking to the people more powerfully than *we* are, and we have to do something to reassert control."

"Dancehall, good or bad?" was a recurring topic in the interviews for this book. Many artists said that the DJs were just fulfilling the role of reggae music as the "voice of the people"—if there is much violence in dancehall lyrics, it is because there is much violence in Jamaican society. Others pointed to the growing number of "conscious" DJs putting out morally positive records over hardcore dancehall riddims. Perhaps most controversial was former police commis-

"NO PICTURES PLEASE . . ."

SELASSIE I

PAPA SAN
"People listen to DJ more than politician..."
New Kingston

sioner Trevor McMillan's announcement of a ban on DJ lyrics that promote violence. This seemed to some artists a throwback to the "rude boy" era of the Sixties, when the government actively censored music and made some songs even *more* popular by banning them. If there was a consensus, it was that reggae music can regulate itself.

In 1994 and 1995 a cultural flavor returned to dancehall-style reggae. Acoustic instruments are being heard again. Two-time Grammy winner Shabba Ranks's new album features a duet with Michael Rose on an old Black Uhuru tune; the now dreadlocked Buju Banton is releasing songs with spiritual themes. Some of the older artists are skeptical, but it appears that dancehall reggae is getting back in touch with its roots.

Papa San

The majority of reggae songs nowadays is dealing with everyday life situation, what is happening on the street—the fussing, the fighting, the war, you know, and starvation of poor people, and politics and all those kinda things, and of the whole system. You know, you have pastor up there preaching to all the people and then doing wrong at the same time. So there's a lot of things that's going on in our eyesight. So you find, it's just an everyday life situation where you ought to listen to and see what to put 'pon a riddim and write about. What I really write about most of all is just, starvation, poor people, hard life, fussin' and fightin', politics, trickster, Mafia, all different kinda things.

I also write comedy stuff to make you laugh, because you have to switch a little and give out to people to cheer up and make them feel nice, because not everybody likes to 'member about the past. Entertainer is a person who have to entertain people, right? And to me, as an entertainer, you can't just do one thing. You can't just talk about the serious stuff alone. You have people who come to stage shows and stuff like that, and some people like to hear cultural lyrics and some people like to hear comedy and some people like to hear gimmicks, some people like to hear you talk fast, some people like to hear you sing. So, you have to be like a mixture of things.

People listen to DJ more than politician now in Jamaica. We have the most power, all over. You hear what DJ says, then people follow. That's the reason why you have to lead them in the right way, in the right path. 'Cause if you lead them to the wrong thing, you have people who go out there and do wrong, you know what I'm saying. There are DJs that do that, definitely. In Jamaica, we are role models for all the teenagers and young people. It's not the way DJs talk have a bad influence on kids, it's what some DJs say that has a bad influence on kids. If you're talking about guns and tellin' the kids to do wrong, then that's bad. But if you are talking about God, liberty, love, caring, that's great.

I and the other DJs in the Eighties, we change the whole style, we don't toast and we don't chant like one time, we put it lyrically, we put it more like a poem, you can read along, there is rhyming, it sounds spicy, you can laugh in between that and that and that, so we change the whole music in the Eighties. But still DJ, we still have to respect all the artists who came first and set the pace, we have to respect that. We listened to the dub poets, Mutabaruka is a very, very good dub poet, and he says a lot of things that are really true. A lot of DJs get inspiration from Mutabaruka, a lot, and also Bob Marley, because Bob Marley was so ahead of his time, Bob Marley was talking in the Seventies about the same things that happen now, so we have to look up to that with respect.

In Jamaica right now, we don't really have a copyright law, so anybody can use anybody riddim, and if a guy do a song and it reach number one on a new riddim, everybody is listening to that song, and that is the sound that is kicking now, everybody will try to use the same riddim to get their song to kick, too. Is a situation where, you know, dog eat dog. You put out a riddim, and everybody wanna ride it, because that's the riddim that lickin' right now, so basically, don't have no copyright law right now in Jamaica, you can't stop those things. I always write my lyrics to fit the riddim. Sometime when you go to the studio and listen to a riddim, the riddim give you a different feeling, you can maybe build a song right on the spot right there. Rap and DJ are comin' together now in the Nineties. The only difference between rap and DJ is the accent, because they speak English and we speak patois. So we've got to DJ our lyrics in patois, they have to DJ their lyrics in their accent. Basically they'd be rappin' in English, and we'd be rappin' in patois, that's the difference. And the next difference is that we use reggae, the hardcore dancehall riddim, and they use the hip-hop, but basically they're the same thing. Rap is comin' after DJ, and now, what they're tryin' to do is use hardcore riddim, dancehall riddim, and make it nicer, and we try to use their hip-hop instead of our hardcore, and try to make

BACKSTAGE AT REGGAE SUNSPLASH
(*left to right*) Little Lenny, Ed Robinson, producer Patrick Roberts
Bob Marley Center, Montego Bay

COBRA
"You cannot ease up . . ."
New York, 1993

it nice, so it's a vice versa thing, you have both sides goin' over, we're goin' over, they're comin' over. I think that is very very nice for all the musician to do.

Reggae music is moving, and you know why it's moving? Because people around the world realize that reggae is something that's good, and it can teach you a lot of things. It teach you how to live, and how to take care of yourself, how to cooperate, how to live as one people who God put on earth, and it teach a lot of good things. It's hardcore, it's raw, and people love that. And then the riddim has a lot to do with it. People love the riddim, it's different, it grabs them first and then they listen to what you have to say. Reggae has been around so long, and it's overdue now for reggae to get a break.

Veteran DJ Papa San has some advice for youths who want to get into the music business: stay in school and get your education first. He was interviewed in Kingston.

"Mad" Cobra

I from a little kid growin' up, I like to listen to, like, the veteran artists, like Bob Marley, you know, he's the foundation. . . . I love to listen to Bob Marley. General Echo, Lone Ranger, Tonto Irie, Charlie Chaplin, Josey Wales, Daddy U Roy. But coming into the past two years before I get a break, my main influence is Ninjaman, you know. Comin' out now I'm soundin' different, you know, I reach where I want to, you know. Right now, I'm lookin' on a bigger thing, you know, I'm thinkin' different, and I sense that not culturally, but lyrically, you know. Slang changes every day, so you have to just build lyrics on new slang every day, that's the way of the reggae thing right now, new trend, very competitive, so you have to just be there with your lyrics, your riddims, and what have you. If you want to be successful, you cannot ease up, you have to be on it every day.

DJ [is] roots music, in a sense. You have, in DJ, reggae dancehall, you have a lot of different classes. You have the DJs who talk culturally, they talk only about reality and consciousness. And next you have the DJ who talk about the girls, some talk about the guns, well, I talk about everything. I vary it, you know, any topic I will deal with, I turn my mind to deal with anything, anytime, anywhere. I have no favorite, it's just what people live, I talk what people live in daily life, that is what I talk. In other words, I'm a messenger.

Right now, they want to get your patois talk, you know. If we were gonna change, like we say "What a gwan?" it would become "Yo, what's up?" It wouldn't make sense that is reggae. "What a gwan," that is reggae, we're talkin' reggae, and reggae only patois—what we know back home, that is what we want to give to the international market, we say, this is what we have to offer. They want to hear reggae, we give them reggae. The riddim change, so be it, but the style is still there.

Right now, reggae, where reggae is at right now, it let me feel real good. Because, looking at myself, like, couple years down the road, I'm looking on movies, like Jimmy Cliff did *The Harder They Come*, Bob Marley done his work, Shabba doing his work, I'm doing mine. . . . What is my wish, that I would like, record companies, or . . . most artists in Jamaica to look at, is to come together and make a show . . . movie . . . saying, this is reggae, this is what reggae is like in Jamaica. This is reggae dancehall in Jamaica. This is the sufferation that we go through in the ghetto. This is where we hope to go, you know. Is showing you that this is what we want to achieve, the struggles comin' up and, you know . . . I've written a couple script already, that is my main aim, and I'm gonna seek help because I want to get that across.

My special message to the fans out there, and what I want this time to get across in my interview, you have some . . . whenever a DJ get into a . . . for instance, me, Shabba Ranks, Buju Banton, Cutty Ranks, Tony Rebel, Capleton, you know . . . we gain certain popularity. International market is lookin' at us, and saying, "We've got to invest in these guys." You have some of the DJs back home, or some little people who, in other words, they don't want you to go, they don't want you to be enlightened, they are talkin' that you switch [styles]. That is bullshit! That is bullshit! Nothin' at all can let me switch from Jamaican. Nothing! The music, they are the ones are saying, Jamaicans are backward, you know, and the international market out there, people, the white folks, and the American, Caucasian get to love our song. You find, down south, people in Africa, they love reggae more. Japan. Canada. Worldwide. And the people see it and, "Yeah, we like this!" And we are ambassadors of music. And we are goin' out there and spreadin' the music, international, and they are saying that these DJs switch.

I'm from the ghetto, I know how to walk barefooted and go to bed without dinner, you know. I know how to go without dinner, I know hard life, you know, can't dress, I know all of those life, and that help me with the support of the people, and I reach somewhere.

JAMMY'S RECORDING STUDIO
Kingston 11

The people respect that and they love what I'm doing, yet still, there are some people who sit down and . . . grudgeful people! What I would like the Jamaican people to know, never, I will never change, I will never rearrange. And I love all the fans in America, England, worldwide, I'm grateful for the support.

Jamaicans, we don't know what we have until we come out of the place and look back, and say, "Boy, this is it," because, we want to go back home. I'm here [U.S.A.] for three months and I want to go home now, you know. Everything is OK, and that is my message to the people out there, I love them, and I hope to put out more hits, and I will be doing that, putting out more hits, hits after hits. Reggae is love and happiness, and we're here and we're happy, and we're one big family.

Cobra was among the first wave of dancehall artists to achieve international popularity in the Nineties. He was interviewed in New York.

Tiger

I turn all kind of things into lyrics. "He's riding a bicycle, he's riding through. Don't hit me darling, cause you might get the blues." "The car parked dere, the cab is square, somebody might lick you from the rear." Everything in life, y'understand. Nature, y'know, and people.

The music change in the Nineties, y'understand. They rough it, rough it up. In five years it change some more. Music will be fully computerized, even the lyrics, they get them digitally. But one thing they can't replace, imagination, pure psychology. I'm up here a long time, I don't worry, I'm-a livin' ahead, thinkin' ahead—I always be two, three years ahead of the rest. When they catch up with me, I'm on to something else. I'm glad for Shabba and the Grammy, but I pass those stages.

Some of the DJ set a bad example for the youth. I'm an entertainer, I'm a comedian, but I don't say what some of the DJ say—I don't tell the youth to look under the young girl dress. I tell them, don't worry, this is your friend Tiger, don't worry, everything will be all right.

So as reggae music now, and improvement, like right now people like me are playing this role, now, which is consistency, good work, and everything, you know. We gotta educate people, still, we gotta educate people as entertainers. What I'm saying is that, it's gonna go so far, I-a

TIGER
"One thing they can't replace—imagination . . ."
Hope Botanical Gardens, Kingston

WILLIE ONE-BLOOD, DEVON D
Kingston, 1992

feels that even people in Alaska, man, North Pole, goin' to be warm to reggae. Japan, reggae big in Japan, really hardcore. Japanese are hardcore and lovin' reggae, man. Japan is doin' a big thing for us. Let me tell you, man, it's goin' to be a beautiful atmosphere, believe me, man, beautiful. That's the way I express it.

Tiger's humor and biting social commentary have won him millions of fans in Jamaica and abroad. He was interviewed in Kingston.

Devon D

As you can tell, a lot of dancehall DJ gettin' signed by major labels. You know that major labels is power; if they keep on doing things like this, then there's no ending to it. You know that Tiger just got signed, and Buju [Banton], that's the next DJ that takin' things to the peak.

PLIERS, SPANNER BANNER, CHAKA DEMUS
Black Scorpio Studio, Kingston

Dancehall music on the whole, you know, drop the quality of reggae music. But you have to do the thing that the people want, and dancehall music is what the people them really want, seen?

Devon D is an independent record producer in Kingston. He was interviewed in May 1992.

Chaka Demus

I think it's going to reach a very far distance. This is just the start of it; I think DJ music is gonna do well. Right now me and Pliers have a tune, it's on the British chart now, "Murder She Wrote." I think DJ music is doing well, but the best is yet to come. We mostly try to deal with love in our music. Bring people together. Reality of life and t'ings. That's the main message of reggae. Bringing people together, love.

BUJU BANTON
"Is a real challenge there . . ."
Kingston

Pliers

Reggae music grow bigger and bigger every year, greater and greater, and it soon take over. Nuff people no expect it really reach that stage. 'Cause reggae music have nuff little lessons that people can learn and all dem t'ing. Different reggae artists deal with other different t'ings, DJ about different t'ings. It's not only about lovers. We have music that say how people get together and live together and all dem t'ing there. We preach all different kinda stories and all different kinda realities, all kinda t'ings, you know, so we going big —we going to reach big.

Chaka Demus and Pliers, who scored an international hit in 1992 with "Murder She Wrote," were interviewed at Black Scorpio Studio in Kingston.

Buju Banton

You approach and ask Buju Banton, do you personally feel the music has changed over the years? I would answer the question, without a doubt yes, I feel so, because the music you hear in the dance hall now is of the type that, there's lotta days people go to the dance hall and just listen to the lyrics, you have to listen. It has changed. It has now become more lyrical, it is now a obstacle to the craft, is a real challenge there. The dancehall nowadays. It has changed, a lot. It's becoming more conscious, more creativity is in place in the musical thing. Lot of the artist them go with the flow, go with the flow, look at the veterans, all the man move, go with the flow, Tiger, straight up, nonstop.

Buju Banton would say to you, I would say the world is in trouble, well it is indeed in trouble, seen? The world is in trouble, that displace everything. I think it's tremendous in the music industry, doors have been opened. We have their undivided attention. Our music reach a place called Japan, we get through right now, seen? I watch this message in the music, don't stop listen to the music, seen?

Buju Banton has had a long string of Jamaican and international hits in the Nineties. His latest record is titled 'Til Shiloh.

Shabba Ranks

People should just accept dancehall as music, you know. Much work has been done by myself to make it possible. You know when you want to reach somewhere, you got to do hard work, you got to work to the best of your ability in order for things to reach the climax. Reggae dancehall was here long time and will always be here, but now is the time that people finally realize that they should just give the music a chance.

The one thing that I want to say about the music is this. The music a broke wide. It's spreading like wildfire, broke wide. Reggae dancehall bigger, bigger, bigger, and better and better, the statement is that only the best is good enough, but where reggae dancehall is concerned, it's not the best is good enough, it's the greatest good enough. Reggae dancehall bigger and better, reggae dancehall should go to Hollywood, you know. Just like how we have rappers in America star in movies, that's how I'd love to see reggae dancehall artists progressing, you know.

Rap and DJ music are comin' together. Shabba and KRS-1 make 1992 classic rock. Two music combine as one to form a body of people is very lovely, and whatever it takes to make the world unite or to make people enjoy themselves with one togetherness, we should try do it because we are the ruler of the earth. God created us to rule the earth. So right now music is the only thing that will unite the world, is the only thing that lives on. It's a big step for the music, two music coming together to form one body, lovely get-together, we love it.

What I want to say to the youth, to all the underage girls them, take your education before you be a mom, before you're pregnant. Stay far away from drugs, drugs kill this earth and takes away all your valuable possessions. Keep the faith—that is the greatest thing of all—keep the faith. Will power, strong mind, and ability—with your ability, will power, and a strong mind, hard work and livicate yourself to what you are doing, then you'll score number one.

International dancehall phenomenon Shabba Ranks, winner of the 1992 and 1993 reggae Grammy awards, released a new live album, Face 1/2, *in 1998. He is also working on a new project with Bobby Digital. He was interviewed in Kingston.*

SHABBA RANKS
"Music is the only thing that will unite the world . . ."
New Kingston, 1992

PATRA
"We just need to come and teach people things . . ."
New York, 1993

Patra

I started first listening to Bob Marley, and in Jamaica, everybody says Bob Marley. Even the kids of today, they've heard of Bob Marley and all of that, but I used to listen to him, and on the female side I used to listen to Sister Carol, Mama Liza, and some old stuff, because those were the stuff that teach me a lot of things, those were the people who really influenced me, but . . . I always love singing a lot, so on the American side I would listen to Tina Turner, Madonna, Patti LaBelle, and on the male side, Alexander O'Neal, a lot of those people, Marvin Gaye. No one in my family can sing; it just comes naturally, I am the only one in my family, and I always wonder, why me, you know?

Jamaican music takes a lot of energy today, you know that reggae music takes a lot of strength. R&B and all those other kinds of music doesn't really have the energy that reggae music has, reggae music have an attitude and a beat, that, once people hear it, they have to move, and it's all about reality. It's popular [in the U.S.] because of the television, and most of the artists get into [video] now, so that's why it's so popular here, and most of the black artists here want to take the Jamaican thing and put it in, to get the flavor.

I would say that rap music comes off reggae, much people don't know that, but listen to the way they come back, every artist now wanna rap like a Jamaican. Lots of people want to talk like Jamaican, and . . . I don't really have much to say about it, music is music, so I would say that every day reggae music comes to the front, because that's the one thing about reggae, it's original. You have to be original and always do things better, but it's still reggae.

The first time the tourists come to Jamaica, all they hear is Bob Marley. You know what? Nothing beats an original and a foundation, and he even worth more dying, people give him his respect. That's why us as entertainers need to change our style; we just need to come and teach people things, 'cause Bob Marley come, he would talk about life. So we need to change our lifestyle, that way, whatever time all of us die off and we see Bob [again] . . . I want to see Bob when I die again . . . we have to just come clean and set example, the example that the foundation have set, we should just take it along the way, don't try to bring it down, try to build it up.

Patra's blend of hardcore reggae, R&B, and funk has resulted in numerous international hits. She was interviewed in New York.

"DOWNTOWN" KINGSTON
Princess Street

"CENTRAL" KINGSTON
Waterhouse district

DANCING IN THE STREET
Maxfield Avenue, Kingston

Cutty Ranks

Reggae music is gonna go very far right now, 'cause you have many young artists right now who are gettin' more trainin' in the business. There's a lot a artist movin' up right now, new artists, and even me as one a the guys who bust out a the pack, after twelve and a half years, but that still no compare with some man who have twenty-odd years and just startin' to come out. I think reggae music goin' to go very far and wide, because a whole heap a message in a these lyrics, especially nowadays. Most of the lyrics guys like me talkin' about right now is reality, understand? Is REAL reality, and it a deal with the aspect a things a go on now. It a focus to right now, it a focus to what goin' on in the world.

My message is that the people have the power. The prime minister or the president don't have the power, because the people put him there. If people come together and organize right now, all a them join up, they can break the barrier. The only way is for people to come together and start live up like a human being, live like a man, and show respect. You see, if every man did have something themselves right now, you wouldn't find so much crime, if every man did have work or have something a do, you wouldn't find so much crime in our country. And what you think build crime? Poverty, and poverty is hungriness, and only thing control poverty, the big man, that is the one who make poverty because them want all, and they want to break up everything.

Me give a warnin' to the big man them, me warn them a stop pressure the youth them. Too much pressure 'pon the youth, that's why the youth them a war and a rob and a shoot, poverty, it a build up crime, and that is not a lie. And yet still some people in the public, some a them no want to listen, but some who are the wise one are listenin', and some a them open themselves to it and start get smart, because when me a talk a reality is not just lyrics, is me heart it come from. Me look and see what go on and me see it clear, clear, clear. Everybody can see what happenin' today, it's a time people them realize what goin' on.

Even some a the artists who DJ about guns, why you think they DJ about guns? It because guns spread all over, all around, guns full up in a Jamaica, New York City, Miami, and the main part of it, 95 percent of the world taxpayer money spent on guns and nuclear bombs, seen? So is reality. DJ music is the new roots right now, it's

CUTTY RANKS
"Live like a man and show respect . . ."
Penthouse Studio, Kingston

the roots that I&I know, it's the same thing that go on for a long, long time, is just that things come out into the open more now. We a see alla them thing out there. Now some people see it, but are afraid to approach it, them scared to approach the aspect a things a go on now, but man like me, I don't scared, if they want to destroy me for the truth, then destroy me, but me no stop talk. That is reality. If you kill me, millions more arise. If the big man destroy me, they only make it worse for themselves. That only gonna make people see it more clear.

I just do my thing and plan my life, and me no plan my life in no two year or three year. No one don't know what comin' in the future, no one don't know what comin' next. No one don't know, but you can prepare yourself for the future, and when you prepare yourself for the future, if good come, it make it much better for you, if bad come, you can face it because you was already prepared. A lot of people don't do that, they have one dollar they eat up whole, and tomorrow they don't have anything to spend, when they could a spend fifty cent and keep fifty cent for tomorrow.

Nuff guys think that in the music business is just money alone, it's not just money alone, it's the principle, how you deal with this thing, and how far you really want to bring it to. Guys like me, we don't come in this business for money alone. I agree, everybody need money, but I mean, I don't come in this business for just money alone, I come in this business to let out certain things what people a hide, what certain big fish hide and cover up, and if I make money, that's fine, and I intend to keep on sendin' the message all through the whole world, and influence the younger generation and the young kids, and make them learn something from me. Thus, when the day come where things get slow for me, them can carry on the tradition. Just like what Bob Marley do, bring reggae music to a very high and far dimension. We as the young artists now come and pick it up from there and carry it further.

DJ Cutty Ranks has released more than eighty records and performed in dance halls around the world since the early Eighties. He was interviewed at Penthouse Studios in downtown Kingston.

Lieutenant Stitchie

I think that the accent that we have, as Jamaicans, is very unique and it attracts people to it, it draws people ... it makes you want to listen to it. Because it's different, and people are not into things that are monotonous, and dancehall music is a different kind of music. It is a form of reggae music—it is not different from reggae music, it is a form of reggae music, just a different time change.

But I think it's because of the exposure that reggae music has been getting through things like Sunsplash, Reggae Sumfest, these various big festivals that are now being televised back here as well as through pay-per-view and other channels, Sting [festival] and all of that. So people are now becoming aware of the music and the energy that it has is, it's very compelling, once you hear it, you have to move.

Another thing that has been happening with this form of reggae music that a lot of you [journalists] have asked about is that reggae music is now being added to mainstream radio, and it's getting a lot of play on the radio, so therefore it is engulfin' a wider market, you know, so therefore that boosts the sale and that expose a lot more artists, rather than the traditional artists that they used to know. Another thing that is also helping is the fact that dancehall music, even reggae music in general, is more used as soundtracks for movies, as well, so you're not only hearin' it on the radio, but when you go to the theater, you're also hearing it in the background, TV commercials as well, that has helped the music in its fullest.

Cross-fertilization—it goes both ways and it is good. Some of the [U.S.] producers, they know what is going down for the small kids, which is very important, but they don't know the [Jamaican] market. And also, you need people that are producin' stuff in Jamaica, because they know that market, and the Caribbean market, which is very important for me, for Stitchie. I will never ever lose the base audience, because they are the ones who make me, and they are the ones who will support me. In order to grow, you need not to let go the known and venture into the unknown, but you need to hold on to what you have got, hold on to the fans that I have, and try to gain new fans. But you still need to have the stuff, the producers in Jamaica deal with the stuff, because Jamaica is where the signal come from, and if you lose, if you lose your base, if you lose your roots, then you're gonna wither. You know?

LIEUTENANT STITCHIE
"Reggae music is the voice of the oppressed people . . ."
New York, 1993

I honestly think when DJs speak about shootin' this and that, some of them, they don't really mean it, it's just a figure of speech, or it's just a way of talkin'. It doesn't mean that they will literally go out there and kill [someone], because they know they are not above the law—no one is above the law, you know, no matter who you are, the president, the prime minister, no matter who you are, the long arms of the law will reach you. So I know that they are aware of that and they are dealin' with their careers, so there's no way that they would go out there to commit crime and expect to excel in their career—it just doesn't work like that.

So when I think that they are speakin' it, it's a way of life, it's things that they see happen around them, because dancehall music is from the ghetto, and I am from the ghetto. Very proud to be from the ghetto, and I'm glad I am from the ghetto. I think that the fact that I am from the ghetto, I see it as a privilege to me, that is how much I love the ghetto and how much I feel about it. Is a ghetto music, is a street music, and you sing what you see happening around you every day. Even the guys from Beverly Hills that want to do the reggae music, they have to come to the ghetto to get the vibes, you know what I mean?

Reggae music in general is a voice for the oppressed people, you know, so that's what dancehall music is all about, so whatever you see happening around, you see man going out there with gun and killin' people and police hunting him, now the DJ talk about it and say he was the one that did that, but he wasn't the one. You know? He's just playing a role, it's just like acting, you know, like in the movie, Kennedy movie, some people act as the assassin and some people act as the president, but they're not the president; it's just a role that they are playing. So is the same thing with the dancehall artist, they're just playing a role. I'm not gonna swear for everyone, but I just know that they are playing a role.

I think badness lyrics goes right across the board in all music forms—calypso, rap, R&B, you name it, dancehall music, reggae music—I think it goes right across the board. And I think we're living in a democratic country where freedom of speech is a democratic right, you know, so we should feel free to say anything as long as it is not instigating any violence against the government—"Go out and kill somebody"—as long as is not instigating, so if a man want to say he did this, is just a lyrics, is nothin' that he will do. But I am not supporting a man go out there and say, "Hey, kill that man because of his beliefs, or because of his thought." I totally detest that. And also,

SECURITY FOR SURETY
Reggae Sunsplash, Montego Bay

I think that there is the law and we have to respect the law. And there is a law against expletives, and profane languages, and I think that we should abide by the law. If you arrest someone, is gonna make them more popular, is like you're building a mountain out of a molehill, but I don't support anyone going on stage and saying, "Hey, shoot police or shoot this one or shoot that one." And frankly, I've never heard anyone go onstage and say, shoot the police, no one would disrespect police, no one, because the law is there to protect us. So, I don't think it's serious.

My hope is that one of the most prestigious awards, the Grammy awards . . . I would like it to be like an on-screen award rather than just a backdoor award. And also, I would like as an artist to achieve in getting reggae music, or dancehall music, being a recipient of the music-of-the-year award, the song-of-the-year award, where it is pooled with all these other songs from all over the world, and reggae comes out the winner as the song of the year, and not just as a reggae category. I hope that there will also be a reggae category in the *Billboard* chart, where you have R&B, you have rap, you know, I'd like to see reggae or dancehall. But that is one of my hopes. I'd like to see more reggae artists being signed to a record company, to major record company, and . . . I have to say this, and I would very much like you to make mention of this, that Atlantic Records is a trendsetter, they're the first one to sign me and sign dancehall artists, and that has opened the eyes for many other record companies to sign all the other acts that follow.

Recording artist Lieutenant Stitchie is a former schoolteacher who now teaches through his music. He was interviewed in New York.

Lady Saw

The dance hall is becoming more positive. It is! The DJs are getting more popular now, because everybody is doing like, hard-core lyrics, lyrics with meaning. It used to be like that, like, years ago when you have the older DJ in those times, they were the ones that were the more cultural DJs, but nowadays, everything, people talk about gun and sex, which people love now, including me, 'cause I talk sex. You know? Dancehall is hot nowadays, real hot, in Jamaica, hot.

Right now, the culture DJs are real strong. You've got Tony Rebel, Beres Hammond—good singer, cultural singer—and you still got Josey Wales and Brigadier Jerry, they haven't done yet, they are still here. We the younger ones tend to deal with, like, some of us DJ about violence, which they're fightin' against now, but people love to hear those kind a music in the dance hall—they are still reality.

I don't really talk about guns and things, 'cause I don't know much about it. I see them, but I don't . . . that's for the men, you know. Sometimes some of them don't know about them either, but they talk about them, in their mind, you know? But right now, it's getting serious because they're fightin' against that and promise to lock us up if we talk about that. I don't know. Some people definitely don't think so, because, let me tell you. What some DJ are talkin' about, gun and police business and police brutality—it do happen, and people have to talk about it, so if they try to silence the DJ, ain't gonna work. 'Cause people need to talk more about that, police brutality and things, and some of them, it's just the music, they just talk and don't mean what they're saying, I don't think they should really take it so far, you know. Right now they are sayin' we, the DJs, are the ones that make people do things—like me, talking sex now, some people say I will spoil the kids and things, but a lot of kids know more than I know.

Every day there is a new talent, a new talent every day, you've got somebody that just cross wicked, good lyrics and things, I mean, I think there is a lot of good future, a lot of good things going to happen in my career, because there is a lot of major company who is interested in me, so I'm choosing which one I want to sign to, and keep doing my work and thing at the best of my ability, please the people, you know, because that's what I'm here for, pleasin' the people.

My message that I'm leavin' now is for people to keep the peace, you know, and no matter how life is hard, just work to the best of your ability and you'll earn what you want, or reach your goal. You just hang on in there and do your thing.

Lady Saw, who named herself after the late singer Tenor Saw, is one of the most versatile of the new breed of reggae artists. She was interviewed at New Name Music in Kingston.

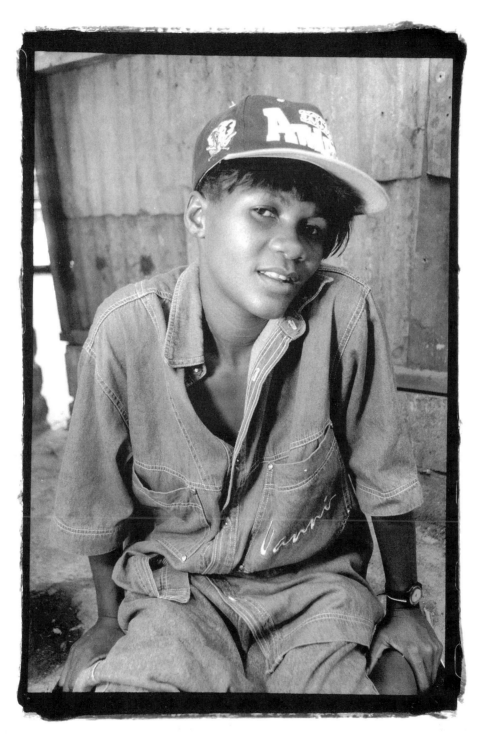

LADY SAW
New Name Music
Kingston

Super Cat

Bob Marley did his part of the work by taking the music inter-nationally, Bob Marley, Peter Tosh, Bunny Wailer, all those people, Judy Mowatt, Marcia Griffiths, Rita Marley, the I-Threes, everybody who was there in that time did their work. So now it's a more smoother road to walk for people who is comin' out of the business, and for expand level. It's more easier for the new artists, although a lot of people don't want to get the situation organized, they are afraid of the ghetto youth makin' money, is true.

As far as I could tell you, reggae in the Nineties, it's collaboratin' now with an international feel, for instance, I'm referrin' to the hip-hop. The simi-larity of this type of music is that, it's the same street people comin' from the ghetto, off the street, singin' the music, 'cause if you notice, the people that doin' hip-hop in America are people that comin' from the mean street of the ghetto, and they're comin' with the same message, they're lickin' out about sufferation within I&I community, the oppression within I&I community, po-lice brutality, and all a them type a thing there. If you want to find ghetto, there is nowhere you can find ghetto, as big as the ghettos in America, so all people them talkin' about ghetto only down in Jamaica don't know what they talkin' about. When you pressure ghetto system, it explode.

Most of these youth you find deejayin' reggae is the youth with Jamaican parents background, or youth who leave Jamaica long time ago and grow up here. But the youth who DJ reggae up here is not gettin' the exposure that they're supposed to get down there in Jamaica. Their records do not play that regular in Jamaica as Jamai-can artists' music play in America. 'Cause you can't pushin' one side of the fence and not pushin' the next side. Everyone is entitled to their respect in the work them doin'. I feel like if Jamaican artists them can come here and eat food and get their exposure, the foreign artists them supposed to get the same exposure down there. Because is up here U.S. dollar isn't the strong dollar, it's the only one. So you have to deal with both sides of the fence.

I see reggae music headin' straight towards mobilizin' these people who don't understand them culture and don't understand where they're from or where they're goin'. 'Cause lot a people today here in America, you tell them that I&I is black African, I&I is African-American, them gonna tell you, no, them is Yankee. So we have to make them know that this music is the foundation and the heartbeat of the people which was scattered abroad in slavery, and this is the music going have to bring I&I together, which is

SUPER CAT
"This music is the foundation . . ."
New York, May 1992

the drum sound, the drum sound is comin' from I&I foreparents' background. 'Cause I&I foreparents bring the drums. Anywhere there was slavery, there was the drum. And we here today, artists and players of instrument, I want them to know that the artistic background is comin' from I&I foreparents, because them no have no bass and guitar in them times, them dance to the drums. Is the heartbeat of the people them here today, scattered abroad, and they have to mobilize themself through this music, because a people without a music could never be a nation.

One more thing I want to say, I want to say to all the artists them out there, I want to say that there is no future in smokin' this crack thing, 'cause I&I know that sensimilla was the foundation and the wisdom of the music. The weed of wisdom is that what I&I appreciate in I&I musical kingdom, I&I know nothin' about this crack thing, this crack thing is a thing that turnin' the people them upside down. I want all the artists them involved in this business know that keepin' away from crack is also keepin' you more successful to the goal that you want to achieve in life.

Recording artist Super Cat was interviewed in New York shortly after the release of his 1992 album, Don Dada. He recently appeared on the massive hit "Fly" with the band Sugar Ray.

PANHEAD (1966–1993)
"Music alone shall live . . ."
Kingston, 1993

Panhead

Dancehall is the roots music now, mostly poor people go for dance-hall music still. Dancehall are the root. Right now you have nuff company a sign up reggae artists, you know, that mean them decide the Caribbean where them invest their money. They no invest their money in a idiot thing. They spending money on a money-making thing. We carry out a message and a thing of money-making. I&I as reggae artists, don't want to deal just with money, we want to bring some change to other people.

The reggae music must go on, you know hard work the key to success. You have man like Bob Marley, and before Bob Marley, so the work must go on from stage to stage. We just have to work and carry it further. 'Cause the way reggae music go, the work of I&I now to continue where Bob Marley and them left off. Music is a whole, music is not for one man, so it up to we, the next generation, to carry it on.

In the past few years reggae take off like a rocket, you know, wailin' in Japan, wailin' in Europe, wailin' in Africa, reggae has spread out. Music alone shall live.

Panhead (Anthony Johnson), one of the most promising young talents in reggae, was tragically murdered in 1993.

PANHEAD
"Dancehall is the roots music now . . ."
Black Scorpio Studio, Kingston

KING JAMMY, PRODUCER EXTRAORDINAIRE
Jammy's Studio, Kingston

SPRAGGA BENZ
Kingston, 1993

CAPTAIN BARKY
King Jammy's Studio
Kingston

WICKERMAN
Black Scorpio Studio
Kingston

YELLOWMAN
"Reggae a move, but some people don't take it serious . . ."
Stony Hill

"King" Yellowman

They claim that the roots is not there, I guess, but it's still there—it's just that our style is different, but it's still reggae. Dancehall, you can still use a dancehall riddim and make it a roots music still, sing a roots lyrics over it, and it nice. That's what Freddie McGregor doin', Gregory doin', Bunny Wailer doin' it, Third World, everybody doin' it. We have dancehall singers, too.

Well, it just goin' keep on change, change, change, you know, a style goin' go on for like a year or two, and the old style comin' back, they're bringin' back the old riddim there, in a dancehall style. They're goin' back to the old Alton Ellis and Heptones and alla them thing there. Me a work 'pon a album and we use live bass, not the computer bass, me and Sly and Robbie, Danny Brownie, Sagittarius Band, me love the real thing, you know, solid. They say our style, now, the dancehall style, it startin' to mix with the hip-hop thing now, so it a change. It sound sweet, you know. It make more people appreciate it, the style of riddim, the hip-hop style, we call it raggamuffin style, them style there a go on now.

You have about four different type a reggae still, which a lot of people don't know—you have the roots style a reggae, which is the Bob Marley style; and you have the dancehall style, which is my style, Shabba, Supercat, Bailey, Charlie Chaplin; and you have another style, which is the pop style, like Ziggy Marley, UB40; and then you have the lovers' rock, like R&B, like Maxi Priest, you know, Beres Hammond. All a them reggae, various different feel a reggae. Reggae a move, but is a some people don't take it serious, like the Jamaicans. It's our music, but them don't take it serious, so some other people have to make it big, like a foreign artist like Tina Turner or Lionel Richie, UB40, all them artists, make it wide.

My message to the youth them, just keep away from drugs and unite with one another. 'Cause I don't give a damn, just deal with it God way and deal with it like people and people. Help each other and love each other and respect each other, you know. Just forget about the violence and thing. The only cure for this world is everybody have to deal with love and unity, have God in your heart, everything cool. Judgment have to come before this world clean up, you know, this world already rotten, so God goin' just have to clean it up and build another world. But fi now, them have to just unite.

One of the originators of dancehall-style reggae, King Yellowman has been touring worldwide for more than fifteen years. He was interviewed at his suburban Kingston home.

Tony Rebel

My audience is the entire world, which is every human being, my audience is not just Jamaican, but at the same time, maybe it is easily understood by Jamaicans because of the language that I'm expressing myself in. My message is not really directed to one special people, and it is international, because we need to tell the world about love, and that we are all brothers and sisters regardless of complexion or whatever, we know that we are all human, and we need to get that message across to everybody.

Jamaican music, this music that is originated here, is the inspired music from the most high. This is the music that God has sent to the people to really bring the message that He wanted to get across to them. I think this music was around long before now. This music was the original music that me and you and all the other people forefathers used to listen to. And maybe because of some unfortunate situation, we was dispatched to different place and don't remember nothing about it. But whenever you hear it again, you can feel it, and that is even greater than when someone come around and teach you about it. That's why they said, "Who feels it, knows it." So that's why everybody can respond to it.

I think those people who are in authority in Jamaica should place some effort around our music, in order to give it exposure, or show that they appreciate and love the way the music is heading. The people who is in authority here, musically, they don't seem to know the significance of the music, or they know but they are not saying. Because there is no other thing in Jamaica bringing in as much tourism as reggae music, bringing as much foreign exchange which the country is in need of so much, and I think they should really do something to upgrade it. They put the least effort around reggae, but it's like, the stone that the builder refuse become the head cornerstone, because nobody promote that thing, they put all that effort around other music, and still, as a late non-starter, reggae surprise everybody down at the final furlong. It is the one that is leading the pack. That show me that reggae is really God's music, some omnipotent power is carrying it along the way.

Right now the people's heart is in the computer riddim, any computer riddim they hear, they just LOVE it. After this get old too, maybe what they're going to do is combine this one now with that old one, and a different sound will come forward. Nobody will get

TONY REBEL 'PON THE MICROPHONE
"We're in a learning process still . . ."
Ocho Rios, 1992

left out, like you who love your guitar in the music, you'll hear a little of that, and me who loves to hear just the keyboard, you know, we can both be satisfied with the sound that is coming across. Everything is just a whole evolution of the music, just like how we used to have ska and rock steady, to the reggae era, and now they're saying it is dancehall, this DJ thing evolve from everything, and maybe down the road something else, you know what I mean? The change is all around, and the change is rapid.

The most important thing in the music is what you are saying, so to get what you're saying across, put it to the kind of music that people like. That's why now you have songs with a crossover, like a little reggae and a little of the hip-hop feel, like Shabba and Maxi Priest are doing now. I think the producers and the entertainers are aware of that, too. People want to hear the words, but they want to hear the kind of music that they like, and we have to listen to them.

People on the whole accept the beat and the melodious sound that you can bring across on the beat. So whether a cultural song or a slackness song or whatever, once you get it across on the riddim that people can dance to, they will accept it. So not because you are singing or deejaying something cultural, why you're going to put it on a riddim that nobody going dance to? When people hear a nice riddim that keep them going, that's the one that they're going to buy, because when people go to party, they want to hear something lively. So that's what I did. I'm in the style just like any DJ, and I'm on the same kind of riddim, but I'm sending a message.

I make songs about everything that is around me. Mostly, I concentrate on the topics that everyone can relate to, particularly economical issues, social issues, everyday life. That's the kind of inspiration I get, that no matter which country you're from, what kind of language you speak, you will want to hear it, even if you don't understand the lyric at the moment, you feel it. If you feel it and don't understand it, you get curious, and then you try to understand it. And once you understand it, you're going to give acceptance to it, because it's referring to you and me and everybody.

I give thanks to Irie-FM, because that's the station that really expose me to a certain level, I and other artists who come out at the same time. Like I was saying, at the beginning, I was recording from long time, but the radio was not giving me justice in terms of airplay. When this station came, they needed songs to play, to have reggae 24 hours a day, seven days a week, actually every artist in Jamaica would get a play, and by playing a certain song and hearing that,

TONY REBEL AT HOME
"We're going into the 21st century now . . ."
Kingston

they thought, yeah, this sound good, and want to play it again. Some of the songs that I was recording before Irie-FM came on sounded new when Irie began to play them, because nobody used to play them before. Well me glad for it, man, that the other station cannot determine what people hear now. Most people now listen to Irie-FM, and more artists are getting a play because of all that. It is having an influence on the other radio stations.

We're going into the twenty-first century now, and artists have to change, even the biggest artists. Maybe even Michael Jackson will have to adjust himself, because people have been hearing too much of one thing from him. If somebody's been doing a certain type of music from the Seventies, and that's what people have been getting from him all this time, then maybe him need to observe his type of music and then make some type of adjustment, with a little of that type that he had before, and a little of the new sounds that the people like.

Five years down the road, you'll be hearing better quality emerging from the music. Within the whole producing fraternity, as far as musicians are concerned, we are in a learning process still. We are still getting new ideas. Nuff of our entertainers, they no play instrument yet, and merely by learning to play instrument and learning some other aspect of the music will help them to be more rounded. Five years down the road, I see that as better for the music. And DJ on the whole, five years down the road people are going to see who are the good DJs, because every minute a new DJ arrives.

I think rap emerge from the DJs here, but now it's started coming back to the roots, you have rap artists who are deejaying, and some popular music that emerge from here is our Jamaican DJs deejaying 'pon the rap riddims. That's a good thing, using the Jamaican style of music on the American riddims. It's like two brothers from the same family, and they went off in different directions, and now they're getting back together again, and that will be more strength. Imagine, it's like the prodigal son return and combine with the brother who stayed at home, and bring all the street information and come on back and share it. You see, the music has reached the four corner of the world now, and it's only a matter of time before everybody a going to get to love it.

Mandeville native Tony Rebel has released numerous records on the Penthouse label and his own Flames Productions. He was interviewed at his home in Kingston.

TONY REBEL AND BUJU BANTON RELAXING AT REBEL'S HOME
Kingston

BEENIE MAN, DANCEHALL SENSATION
New York, 1997

SHINEHEAD REHEARSING
New York, 1991

BARRINGTON LEVY
Kingston, 1992

TERROR FABULOUS
New York, 1994

Daddy Lizzard

Reggae has gone international, that's all I know. Nothing can stop reggae, 'cause everybody love reggae. The foreign artist have been takin' up reggae, so why not we take up hip-hop? Everybody is into reggae, so is best we just get involved in hip-hop, too. Jamaican people goin' for it. I recently done a song for Bobby Digital on a hip-hop riddim and it sound good. They don't know what category to put reggae in now, because reggae is above almost everything now, they have it mixed now, so when some people who don't like reggae, and they hear reggae hip-hop, they just go for the hip-hop part. But is still reggae. And who don't like hip-hop, they just go for the reggae part. But they still havin' hip-hop. That's what I like with crossover reggae, it make everybody come together, everybody enjoy the music.

I've been to Japan in the last year, and reggae is very big. Surprise me! I've been to the show, all I can see is Japanese head, place packed, every show, sometimes they have to keep double show, Friday night, they schedule for one show, when show sell out, they have to keep another show Saturday night, because everybody couldn't hold in the first show.

All the artists them have to do is work very hard, like we once workin' at certain level, now we have to work extra, 'cause you know nuff more things inna the reggae for we. So let us keep workin' harder and harder. Cannot sit and skylark no more, seen? Have to work. You have to be creative, because plenty artist is in the business and everybody come with somethin' new.

It easier for the upcoming artists, because we lay the foundation. Brigadier and Daddy U Roy and Josey Wales and Charlie Chaplin make it fi we, and now we make it for the upcoming artists. Josey Wales, Daddy U Roy, Brigadier, and so forth make it easy for we, because they went through the hardest part of it, now we get a slightly easier part, but the ones after us get it more easier and the one after them get it easier, because the gate is open. The road is paved, no rocky road, everything is smooth. No?

For the youth, one thing me can tell the youth them, let us unite and live lovely. Everyday people get up a kill them one another over one little simple thing every day. Me just a beg them to stop, live good, and make reggae music flow around the world.

In his interview Daddy Lizzard also paid respects to fellow artists Red Dragon, Flourgon, Buju Banton, and Sanchez.

DADDY LIZZARD
"Cannot sit and skylark no more . . ."
Devon House, New Kingston

FISHER DREAD
"It come from the blood, seen?"
Kingston, 1992

Fisher Dread

Yes, from Bob drop out, is like music kinda change still. Right now inna my sight, what Bob used to talk in I music, only the DJ them nowadays, the DJ them on the whole talk what Bob used to talk in I music them. The singer them nah really sing what Bob used to talk, only the DJ them right now me see a do that. The music, it kinda change up. As you know, different taste, different people, you understand, so everybody have to do them own thing, 'cause there is a market for everything. Too much separation a go on in the music thing right now, entertainer fight with entertainer, entertainer complain him bigger than entertainer and him better than entertainer. No want that to go on. That keep the music down, and that me no want.

If we see a man bruk out how like Buju Banton bruk out now big, all we have to do is just go behind him and strengthen him, till one a our time come to bruk out and the rest a stay behind me and strengthen me, 'cause my time a come fi bruk out, we no have to fight 'gainst Buju, we don't want, that's not the business. 'Cause, you see the music now, it a get nicer and nicer every day, reggae music a get sweeter and sweeter every day, and better and better every day. So just wan' keep up the standard, me ask the people them, me ask all a the people them, from promoter to artist right down, alla them, producer, alla them, we ask them to keep up the business, keep it up strong, seen. Every time that a man move, there's a step for we to walk 'pon, seen? So every man have a step to walk 'pon. Just wait 'pon your turn. The line long but wait 'pon your turn. You must reach up a the front to go up on the step. Wait. Yeah man. 'Cause Bob long comin' up, and Bob wait a feel time till him comin'. And he reach a step and go up there and set the foundation. So just we to follow after the foundation and move the right way.

You see the next five years, we a goin' to have some wicked entertainer come, 'cause believe you me, more time me go up 'pon some corner, some little baby youth a DJ, me can't believe, me have to stand up and listen them, as a big DJ, stand up and listen them, yeah man, them bad like yaz, man, me a go listen them, so you see the next five years, cho, them can talk to reggae fans and reggae artists. The Bible done tell, you know, singers and instrument player must run the world. Music on the whole come to the level, must run the world, nothin' else, no politics, no folly tricks and them thing, can't run the world. Music must have to run the world.

'Cause music free Mandela, and nuff people sing to free Mandela, so you know. Music free Mandela, you know, music free Mandela. That why me vexed when me see them bring Mandela come a Jamaica and bring him go in a stadium go lock him up and people get a shot. Yeah man, me vexed man, Mandela should a walk up and down in a Jamaica man, and go in the corners and cribbies and mek man cook banana and dumplin' and butter cake and see what we a deal with down here. Yeah man, for real man. So, reggae music, it a the backbone, for real, man, reggae music a the backbone.

Me never really get downhearted yet, inna the music, from the crowd, me never get downhearted from the crowd 'cause me is a performin' artist, me practice and perform. Practicin' a me house, in front a me mirror, make a some move in front a me mirror and see if that look good. Then me go out in front of the crowd and make all them move. Performin' on the whole is a something we're a born with. 'Cause me father meet me mother 'pon stage, me father and mother was a dancin' partner before them becomes friend and make a relationship and we can come forth, them was a dancin' partner 'pon stage.

It come from the blood, seen? 'Cause General Trees me nephew, me big sister son, General Trees, yeah. A blood thing that run through the vein, from the root a come up, yeah. You see, performin' on the whole, I see Admiral Bailey and Tiger and San, me love how them perform, them energetic, me love energetic artists, me love when artist very much energetic, and me patternize after them artists, me not gonna go 'round the corner and say me no patternize after those artists, 'cause me love all them artists, them move on stage. When your lyrics a no say nothin', make some move say somethin', man. Show some motion. Get to amazin' them. That a me desire, man, a to go up on stage and make people feel nice. 'Cause me love when people enjoy themselves, and me love enjoy myself, and if somebody is there and Jah makin' me enjoy myself, me no want to half enjoy myself, me want a whole. So me love them artist them, Tiger and Bailey and them man. All over the world, them good, every time them come, them come fresh, you know.

Respect to every other entertainer. One thing me still a tell them, wait 'pon them turn, you understand, 'cause it there for them, just wait 'pon it, and just give me some more love and some more unity in I business.

Fisher Dread was the featured DJ on the 1992 Ziggy Marley single "Stop Joke."

SINGER-SONGWRITER WOODEY NOBLE
King Jammy's Studio, Kingston

Brian and Tony Gold

BRIAN: Reggae is a very powerful kinda music. I've traveled all over the world and I notice, once people hear a reggae song, there's a little magic, a little magnet that just draws it to them.

We want to make money, but that's not the main issue. We're not into it to make money. We wanted to uplift the music, you know, so that's why we have to do our best and get a certain sound that can capture the world. And try to bring the message of love across to everybody. Europe and Japan, those places are getting a chance to see it now, MTV and all that, thanks to Shabba and Maxi Priest and Papa San and Burning Spear and all those people.

Well, right now, we're going to be working on our album. It should be out by middle, end, of summer. That's what we're concentrating on. We're doing some shows locally and overseas, and keep rehearsin' and keep makin' music.

TONY: Reggae in the forefront of all the other music right now. I feel reggae is going to be number one kind of music very soon. R&B was the number one kind of music, reggae is going to be. If the music was gettin' the same kind of push five years ago like it's getting now, it would be the same. The promotion there in the music, now it's getting that kind of promotion so it's just taking off.

What amuses me, like in Japan, you see a person that don't know a word in English, but they sing along word for word. That is what amazes me. And it goes right along with the power of the music, you know, that's how powerful the music is. Reggae keep moving upwards, as long as it stays clean. No downward trends, just up, you know.

We want them to really cut out the slackness. Just make everything clean, and for everybody to listen to, whether young or old. And just give the music the support that it needs, so it can reach where everybody want to see it, the highest level that it can go. It's on the way there, definitely.

In addition to their own successful records, Brian and Tony Gold have produced hit songs for numerous other reggae artists. They were interviewed at Jimmy Cliff's rehearsal studio in Kingston.

BRIAN AND TONY GOLD
"There's a little magnet that draws them to it . . ."
Kingston, April 1992

GARNETT SILK (1966–1994)
"Music has to lift you up . . ."
Tony Rebel's yard, Kingston

Garnett Silk

I'm a singer and songwriter; I can DJ, too. "Christian Soldiers" is the latest thing I have out, it's getting a lot of play, it's on the RJR charts. It's done by me and Tony Rebel. We used to DJ together upon a sound called Destiny Outernational in Mandeville, where we both come from. I start concentrating on singing only recently, but I keep up with the deejaying.

Most of the songs that I sing are written by me. I work at different studios, Penthouse, Mixing Lab, Digital B. Sometimes I get riddims built specifically for a song, other times I might hear riddims and find something to put on it. It depends on the vibe. I always feel there is a specific song for a specific riddim.

I write about the things that I see, even in vision. Y'understand? Things that naked eyes can't see. I say Jah set me up to sing only about the truth. Me see myself as an instrument of Jah. I am here to teach and comfort people. I am here to make people happy. Me sing and make people happy, forget their troubles. So there is a common thing about all musicians. All the energies arise from the same place.

Knowing that the reggae is so powerful, people like I&I, like [Tony] Rebel and many others, like Bob Marley, we know the power reggae have, and we know why Jah have the music for, and we make sure we deal with it in the right way, because it is very much influential. So we make sure we don't deal with it in a way that would displease the Father, or even displease the souls of the people, because something might seem nice to a one today, and tomorrow it make him so bitter. So you have to check it on a higher level. So we know the power reggae have, and Jah give us the power, so we must choose it wisely to deal with certain things. Music is my life. It doesn't matter what country or whatever the name of the music, as long as the artist that sings it has a positive spirit. You have some songs promoting destruction and things like that, and I think music has to lift you up.

Yeah, Bob make it clear that if you gonna deal with it, deal with it *right*. Bob's music is a revelation, man, and judgment, and his works help prove what Jah say are true, that God is everlasting, that anything you say and do for Jah, it is everlasting, you can't dead. Whatever you say and do lives on. So Bob is a revelation and a living judgment. Him help reveal the truth of Jah.

Singer and songwriter Garnett Silk, who was one of the fastest-rising and most promising young artists in reggae, died accidentally on December 9, 1994 in a fire at his family home near Mandeville. He was interviewed in February 1992.

SINGER/SONGWRITER LEHBANCHULEH (NORBERT CLARKE)

SINGER AND DJ MIKEY MELODY

DANCEHALL STYLE AN' FASHION
Backstage, Reggae Sunsplash, 1991

CHANNEL 7 SOUND SYSTEM
"Live and direct . . ."
Snake Hill, St. Catherine

Cultural Roots Version

When we started this project, the dancehall explosion had just begun and the picture for traditional "roots reggae," at least at the moment, was bleak. "I don't see any roots lately," said Burning Spear in press notes accompanying a 1992 album. "People have strayed from the roots, from the original understanding." Veteran acts like Spear, Culture, Bunny Wailer, Toots and the Maytals, Wadada, and the Mighty Diamonds were finding more acceptance and respect in Europe, North America, and Japan than they were "down yard." Top-notch back-up bands like Roots Radics and musicians like Santa Davis, Horsemouth Wallace, Skully Sims, and Fully Fullwood were finding studio dates fewer and farther between. The "dancehall Don" and the computer riddim had pushed them all aside.

Several years later, roots reggae has not only survived, it is stronger than ever. There are probably many reasons for this. Many roots artists tour constantly, some in parts of the world that are not reached by major popular music tours; this has the effect of continually broadening the market for reggae in general. Although dancehall has penetrated the U.S. urban market, roots reggae has been steadily building a global audience for years. The boom in "reissue" CDs and boxed sets has resulted in wider distribution of many classic reggae titles, sending listeners in search of new work by the same artists and creating demand for new releases. The growing impact of small record companies such as RAS and Heart-

BUNNY WAILER LIVE
"Put down somethin' that you can relate to twenty years from now . . ."

beat on the international market is measured by the number of roots artists who establish long-term relationships with these music-friendly labels rather than with the fickle "majors."

If there has been a "return to the roots" in dancehall reggae lately, it's largely because the roots artists remained sensitive to their audience and held true to their original vision. A generation of new roots-oriented groups like the Mystic Revealers has appeared; veteran artists like Michael Rose, Junior Reid, and Israel Vibration have released some of their best work in years. Some of the old branches have withered, but new branches have grown. The roots still live.

Bunny Wailer

I don't think it's any part of the artists not coming through, you know, it has to do with the media. If the media tend to push these new types of records that they're making now, based on the promoters that choose to do these kinds of recordings, and then you are in a situation where some people are getting paid, payola in any form, to do these things, to push these records, then they are gonna do that, and that's what's been really happening. And you find that it's a easy route and people tend to always want to take the easy route to make money, they don't want to find themselves doing too much work.

You find that all of this adds up to where the music is not as presentable as it was, and it's like people start gettin' lazy because there has been so many strong foundation that has been laid with the music, and people think that they can just go and live off these old records and the old rhythms without even bothering to go back and lay new rhythms. Out of that, and that's because of the strength of reggae music, because these rhythms, somehow they never die, and the generation that comes relates to these rhythms, and they enjoy them the same way as the generation before did. So you find that out of that, is the easy way out, easy way of makin' money, you spend less and you make more, and then—is not that you make more, but you might make a faster buck—and after that the record dies, which, that's not good, because you don't have anything to put down.

You have to put down somethin' that you can relate to twenty years from now. But the records that are being made now, they die twenty days from now. So, it's really, it makes people start to wonder what's really happening. And then, the old-time religion, the old-time reggae music, is still being played by the artists that have been playing them, but because of the situation where the media tends not to deal with that kind of music, because that's music that's put together properly, arranged, directed, and produced, and then people are not gonna want to pay a guy to play something that you already put so many hours in, you know, hard work in. And then, because of that, guys get spoiled already by people who walk up to them and give them money to play the little lesser side of the music, they are reluctant to push that part of the music, and the lesser side gets really dominant and crowds the greater side of the music.

I know that reggae has been doing its work, and the taste that has been put in people's mouths, and the message that has been put in people's minds, the real authentic reggae music, roots music, I don't think what is happening now could erase that taste. It's just a matter of choice. If you see something good, you always tend to want to do that, you're not gonna go after anything that spoils that.

You know, people always want to be in the limelight of things, in the happenings of things, without knowing or wondering or even trying to find out if it's the best thing for them. People get carried away, and more people get carried away, and more people get carried away, and then people are living in situation where, although the thing might not have been as solid as it should be, it's the thing. It's a new generation, and this generation is gonna go for their type stuff. It's lollipop stuff. It's like, after you have graduated, you're not going to be wanting to go back to eighth class lessons. That's what it is with the music. Because we have come so far, and we are educated within the music, and we have become so sensitive, and know what good music is, and the principles that go with that music, we are not gonna be easily influenced into this new one, because we have already graduated. But then again, if you are a musician, or if you are a listener, or if you have anything to do with music, then you have too high a standard to relate to A-B-C music, because that's the generation, that's the class that is now comin' up. So as a teacher you would still have to find yourself, although you know better than A-B-C, you'd have to be dealing with A-B-C, because that's what's happening.

So, you know, it's a matter of understanding what's happening, and if you can get into it and try to deal with a more positive direction, so that the students can understand that there was a principle that was set that govern the music to the extent that it could have served long enough for them, to come to find that they could just be playing with it the way they are and going as far as they want to go. It never gets boring to them, it never gets stale to them, because that same rhythm is so powerful, it has been laid down in such a strong way that they can't really do anything, they can only play on it and fool around, but those foundations are set. I think it's a great thing for reggae music on the whole, because it's a branch, and sometimes some things stagnate, some things grow. When something branches out, it gives life to the whole.

It's just for the original people that have been in the music to realize their responsibility and not get carried away or get disappointed in any way and find themselves frustrated, going back instead of forward. We have to pay some attention and give some direction, and then, with that we can relate to all sides of this music, because it's a great music and it should be respected and treated that way. And that if we do that, if people know better, at least that would be a good start for giving some direction to the now generation who think that what they're doing, that's the right thing.

I still believe that there are so many people that have been now acquainted to reggae music, that I think it's the greatest music in the world. There are so many people that are professionally earning their bread, surviving, from reggae music, that there's no music right now that you could put with reggae music, in comparison to reggae music, that is doin' the same thing. And there are so many people who still is going to be wanting to have something to do with reggae music, who are just learning to get into reggae music, and who have now learned reggae music to the extent that they are trying to enjoy the different glories of reggae music, you know, so I think it's the music of this century and maybe the next, until we see another one come, but reggae right now is the music of the century.

There are people who are putting the new ideas forward, which are gonna be new compared with all the other ideas that have been put out. That's what's gonna keep this thing alive. Young people gonna see this and they gonna get a new direction. That's our job. Our job is to make it as plain and as strong as we can, so that it serves the new generation, and that they have something to improvise on and take it further. You do that strong, and stretch out.

Bunny Wailer, the original member of The Wailers with Peter Tosh and Bob Marley, won the 1995 reggae Grammy award for his album Crucial. *He was interviewed in May 1992.*

SUNSPLASH MASSIVE

Earl "Chinna" Smith

Reggae have so much to say right now, you understand, we have so many different vibes right now, so we need to support this. Every one of them vibes that don't work, economically, an integral form, so that we keep them whole and at least compose and come up with that kind of music, it can live, and many can get them satisfaction from the message that them make out through the music, and also the benefits.

So, you can't put down digital music, you have to love all of the style, all of the branches of the roots. It's nice, you know, Shabba Ranks's music, and Ninjaman and all the rest of them, man. The way the music go, it have certain vibes, you know. If you penetrate the music, music is an art, it is for everyone, little joy, little sorrow, everything. Just as I praise Him in the voice, you have to praise Him in the dance, too. You have to dance to the music, it's very important. The riddim will be just nicer and nicer, and no one can know the

EARL "CHINNA" SMITH
"You have to love all of the branches of the roots . . ."
Bunny Lee's studio, Kingston

heights and the level it can reach, you know. The writers and everyone must keep going strong still.

Reggae in the Nineties call for different lyrics, everybody get busy
now, more busy writing, to me the music is getting more serious now.
Playin' the music, everybody is aware of certain things, more the value of
the music. Today you don't hear artists complainin', so much like back in
the Sixties and Seventies, everybody gettin' ripped off and alla that side of
story, because they're more aware of taking care of themselves. So them
don't have to worry, them can bring out certain things without trippin',
and that's good, yeah mon. That's why I&I have to love Bob, because he
talk and prophesy, reassure everyone, him awaken them on how you
should be.

*A musician's musician, guitarist and producer Earl "Chinna" Smith has
worked with literally everyone in reggae music since the late Sixties.*

ZIGGY MARLEY
Bob Marley Museum
54 Hope Road, Kingston

"Bredrin X"

You see a little man, you see a man a pushin' cart 'pon the street, this a man tells me him is a DJ. You see a man him a work in a office, him is a DJ. Every little man right now is a DJ. Y'understand? Any little man who get him hand 'pon a riddim is a DJ. You don't have a professional, really, a man just a set up "Yah yah yah yah" and it sell, y'understand.

You have a little man, know, all him want is a couple note on synthesizer and electric drums, and 'im go in the studio and create a bag a foolishness, understand.

That's why, I don't call them *producers*, I call them *reducers*. I don't call them producers, because they don't know nothing about music, they're not on key. You listen to a lot a them, they're off key.

A music isn't complete unless it have a bridge. You have some DJ riddim, they are two chords; some DJ riddim, they are four chords. If it don't have a bridge, it's not music, y'understand?

"Bredrin X" is known to many in the Kingston studio scene. He asked not to be quoted by name.

Judy Mowatt

When Bob Marley pass, the music took a downhill turn, where things change for the worse; there wasn't anything that Bob Marley stood for, they wanted to defeat the purpose, I mean the forces that be, because they allowed it. And there was a lot of slackness being projected in the music. Yellowman came after Bob pass, everybody was clamoring over Yellowman, but the lyrics was not upliftin'! Bob's music uplifted the people to a certain moral standard, and so when Yellowman came, he took them from that level, whoever he could take down, he took them down. Whenever there is a DJ that is very popular, you find that young DJs come up and relate to that DJ, so other young DJs were coming up and were following the image and the pattern that was set by King Yellowman. And it happen and it happen and it happen and . . . radio stations were playing in Jamaica, radio stations, a certain disc jockey especially was playing that kind of music on the radio, and at that time singers were dethroned. I mean, you can't dethrone a singer, but for a while, it was just DJ. DJ was reigning.

DJ style will live forever, because it is the voice of the people, and a lot of people cannot sing, but they can talk, so this is why they gravitate to the DJ style, and the DJ style is really potent, it's very powerful, and the riddims that they choose, the style that they choose, the riddims that they use are rock steady riddims that people were familiar with before. And so, it's a combination of the riddim and what is being said.

But I have found now that things are changin', they're going through a whole cycle, and we are back to its original, where it's supposed to be. The people don't want to hear the slackness anymore. The people cannot take the slackness anymore, because we are living in an era where people's backs are against the wall, people are going through all different kind of crisis, and they need to hear music that is relating to what they are experiencing. They need the cultural message to uplift them, to take them out of the turmoil that they are in, and find solutions for their future actions.

I have found the dance hall the rallying point for the people, the rallying point where the message for the people—it's like a church, and the congregation goes to the dance hall because I find the DJs today are talking about God, they're talking about cultural topics, they're talking about social topics, and the things that they are

JUDY MOWATT IN CONCERT

talking about is really relating to the people. Upful lyrics. So I am seeing a positive change, and I am really happy.

Being an elder in this business, I know that I have to pass on what I've learned, what I have demonstrated over the years, I have to pass it on to the younger generation. Because it's their turn. They're appealing to the youth. They are the ones that are appealing to the youth, and so I have to combine my efforts with them so they can pass on the energy and the vibration to the youth that are listening to them.

What has happened is that the musicians and the artists from yesteryear, I don't think some of them are conscious of what they have done, but they are passing the baton, it's like a relay race, and you have to pass the baton on. And they have created a platform for today's DJs with the music that they provided in that era. Without them, they would be nothing. Alton Ellis, Ken Boothe, Marcia Griffiths, Bob Andy. These singers today, and DJs, they are drawing upon the work of the artists of that era. And I must say, give thanks for those artists in that era, because if it wasn't for them, these artists today wouldn't have a platform to stand on.

The younger generation need to know about what took place in the time before them, so I like the old riddims. And I like it because . . . what we are giving them is a piece of what we enjoyed. But what I want them to do more is to create. You can listen and you can use as much as you want, but please create, because if you don't create, then you are not providing for the generation after you.

It's a cycle, it goes around and it comes around. The live music has more life, it has more fire, it burns more, you know what I mean? It burns within your heart, it touches your heart. I don't find the computerized riddim moves you like the real music, when the musician uses his hands and feet, it's from the person and not from . . . the fingers and the machine, you know what I mean. What we want in this time is the life of the music, and so we find that the kids today are gravitating to the live, and I'm glad that they have found the lifeline, because they were experimenting with the computerized, but they didn't know the real thing, and now that they have found the real thing, that's what they want.

You notice, on the CDs, they are putting the old stuff on CD, and people are gravitating toward it. In those days, the Ethiopians, the Melodians, the Wailers, what they were doing, they were exposing what existed in their time. Every event that took place in Jamaica, they were like the journalists that covered the event. Music is like the

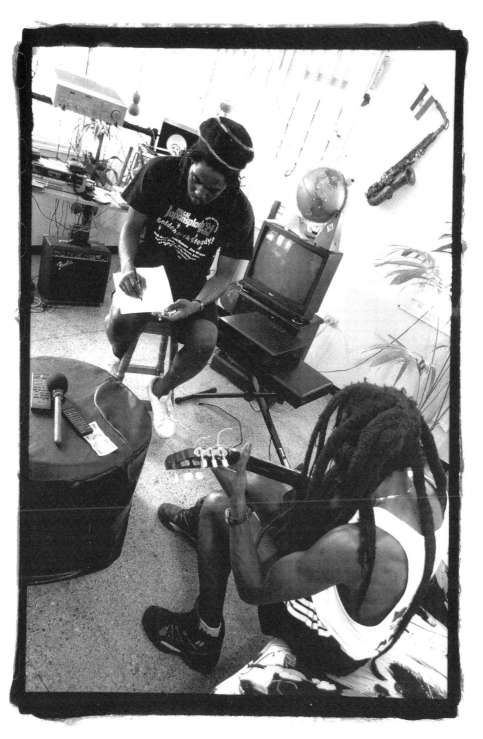

YAMI BOLO AND CHINNA SMITH
Songwriting session, Kingston, 1994

people's news in those days, they were like the people's news. People in England would say, "What is happening in Jamaica? We hear Bob Marley with 'Burning and Looting Tonight,' 'Three O'Clock Road Block,' what does that mean?" That the police are stopping the people—they're having roadblocks in Jamaica now, police are stopping the people, and there's a check from the airport to western Kingston, and you have to beware, because Bob Marley tells you that. Like you pick up the newspaper and read what is happening in Jamaica, it's a semblance of what the artists will sing about.

I don't like when [the DJs] boast about themselves; I like when they talk about what's happening. What we want to hear—I think music is information, communication, education, and this is what we have to understand, is that what we are doing is that we are transmitters, and we are transmitting what we have learned to the people. We are transmitting what is. You have the print media, you have the electronic media, but music is also another medium of communication, and it's the highest and the widest medium of communication because it crosses all barriers, all boundaries.

I was at Tony Rebel's birthday celebration in Mandeville, and I performed, and it was a night of cultural experience, it was a cultural explosion, and everyone was really able to relate what Malcolm X said, what Marcus Garvey said in their message, they were able to relate what Bob Marley said, they were able to relate what His Imperial Majesty said, they were able to relate what is happening in the world today, world events, global events. When you left the concert and you saw some people going to church, because they were dressed for church, and a youth said, "I am coming from church, because I got everything I wanted to know; I learned about God, I learned about what's going on in the world, I know how to relate to my brother man, my sistren, my woman at home, because everything was taught to me in that concert."

I'd like to say to the youths today that it is very crucial, 'cause we're living in a crucial age. We're living in the end age, where we know that God told us in the Bible that He is coming soon, and He also told us the signs, what we were to look for in the end days, children having children, wars upon wars, rumors of wars, pestilence and famine in diverse places, and also earthquake in diverse places, and we see everything manifesting. We know of homeless people and we know that there is no guarantee to our lives—you have a job today and tomorrow you don't, you find yourself on the street if you don't have a job, 'cause you can't pay your rent, you can't buy food, nothing. You are an executive today and tomorrow you are a homeless person.

So, who do we put our trust in, ourselves, or in man? No. The president cannot save us, the clergies cannot save us, the soldiers and police cannot save us. It is God almighty, that never sleeps, that never slumbers. He's the one that is watching over us, and He sees all things, and it is His time. Now is prophecy time. Now is revelation time. And what we have to do is pray. We have to align ourselves spiritually to the Father, because if we don't, as Marcus Garvey said, only the fittest of the fittest will survive. And the weak will perish.

So there can't be any weak heart in this time. We have to be strong. And our strength can only come from one source—spiritual source—from the almighty God.

From back-up singer with Bob Marley and the Wailers to respected solo artist, Judy Mowatt is one of the most distinctive voices in reggae music. She was interviewed in January 1994 in Kingston.

SINGER-SONGWRITER YAMI BOLO
Leggo Studios, Orange Street, Kingston

Yami Bolo

Most time people love livin' in a fantasy instead of in reality, so you have some people that goes for cultural music, and you have some people that goes for sex music, and you have some people that don't go for no music; they go for the money. So it is all mixed up between the whole protocol of Babylon within the system. It's like, as I say, the changing of the guards and the cleaning up of culture, music.

The music speak for itself and it take its own course and direction. Reggae music can only get bigger and bigger, 'cause it big done already—Bob Marley done establish it, and many more great singers, like Junior Delgado, Augustus Pablo, Jimmy Cliff, and man like we, we are trying to really take it to the next dimension, Jack Radics, that whole crew, seen?

So reggae a just get big, big like a dreadlocks on the Earth, the Planet Earth; that mean if a guy love it or not, reggae a just get big, and bigger and bigger and bigger like dreadlocks on the Planet Earth, yeah! So that a really the future of reggae.

Roots singer Yami Bolo's latest recording was Wonder and Sign, *released on VP Records.*

Denzil Williams (Wadada)

We grow up in the community of Trench Town, from early days, and this a place where life, economical life, is very, very hard for the inhabitants. Music is a way for us, we could really sing and really achieve fame out of the singin'. There were artists all around, groups like Wailers, Gaylads, Maytals, Heptones, duos like Alton and Eddie, Higgs and Wilson, Simms and Robinson, y'understand, Alton Ellis and his sister Hortense Ellis, groups like the Schoolboys, the Schoolgirls, Wailing Souls—all from Trench Town. It is a place just full of artists, and you know artists have friends all the while who are around them. So we just become a part of the singing business, just from being around, and form the group in 1980, '81.

Reggae music is the heartbeat of a people, the message of a people. That mean reggae music is a real music, because it comin' from the heart. The beat is synchronized with the beatin' of the system within, comin' from way, way down. It's real music, it's heartbeat music, the pulse of a man. Reggae music have that way down depth, it's so natural 'cause it's

WADADA (Denzil Williams, Kenneth Roxborough, Franklyn Thompson)
"The message of Wadada is love . . ."
Kingston, February 1992

coming from way down in the heart of a people. Livin' conditions, the voices in life, experience, man, practical experience, man, feelings, everything come out in reggae music.

Otherwise, reggae mean "message from the King," and most of the artists them worship Rastafari, so, the music is the King's message. "Ras," in Amharic language, in Ethiopia, mean head. "Tafari" mean creator. So when you say "Rastafari," in Amharic language, you're sayin' "Head Creator." And "Wadada," in Amharic language, mean "Love."

So, as Wadada, our message is clear to the world. Our message is love, what we have to offer to the world is love, because only love can conquer. War cannot conquer. War is not the answer, it's only love can conquer in this world.

We are Jamaican people, we know people are important, regardless of color or creed. We no deal with that, we just deal with humanity. A man is a man, we just accept him as a man. If he have on a pants and shirt, we see him as a human being, regardless of clothes, y'understand. We just deal with him as a human being. We love people and we deal with people, and we welcome people, because the world have to communicate, and we have to communicate with people, of all creed and color and race. That is our policy in reggae music.

Denzil Williams is a member of the roots harmony trio Wadada, along with Franklyn Thompson and Kenneth Roxborough. Their album, Take a Stand, *was produced by Bunny Wailer.*

Ken Bob

The Bible speak, "As it was in the beginning, same shall it be unto the end." So it's like even with garments, sometimes it's like the old-fashioned style comes around again. What goes around comes around, and same as it was in the beginning, it shall be in the end. Because in the beginning it's original. It's like a plant, a tree, the roots which is original, that is the beginning, grows up into the branches. You can try doin' a lot of things, emphasize a lot of things, but the original, the roots, remain. I like the natural music, it's like bein' in the country, you've got your acoustic guitar, you sit down and you play, it has the natural feel. Natural music.

KEN BOB
"In the beginning, it's original . . ."
Kingston Waterfront

I spoke with a director from a company in Japan, and he was saying that the same youths that go crazy for the dancehall, they are turnin' now for culture, you know. Culture. *Roots*. Everything have its place, like they say, everything have its season, right? And we're not here to fight against music, because music is international, whether it's funk, jazz, blues, whatever. Like in Jamaica we don't have any snow, but we don't fight against snow, snow is in your country, so we don't fight against no music. Every music have its own place.

Take, for instance, dancehall music. Dancehall music can be message as well as just pleasure. How I see music, there is serious music and there is pleasure music, like you're workin' six or seven days a week and when that is through, you just want to get up and dance. And then there is another music that can lift your spirit higher and that can aid your meditation. I might feel like listen some reggae, or maybe I feel like listen some African music, or maybe I feel like listen some American music. Because whether the musician is black or the musician is white, we are one, it is music, it is a human being, it is a man, or it's a woman—there is no separation with color or nothing. There is no music separation. It's just like alcohol or food, you can have too much drink or too much food, so you need a little of this, a little of that, a mix-up of the whole thing.

You know if you are seeking for something, like sometime I can wake up and I don't feel too good, and I can read a chapter for the day, Psalms or whatever, something comforting, nice words, comforting to me and then I feel better. I might feel in the mood like listen some Culture, or I might feel like listen some Bob Marley, or I might feel like some Burning Spear or some Diamonds, those kinds of music are spiritual, and man shall not live by bread alone, man shall not live by food and clothes alone, but spiritually, man need spiritual things, too. Seen? So it depends on what you want, you might feel like dancing, or maybe it's a birthday party or whatever, you have music for different time, it depends on a person.

One thing I don't listen to at all, I don't play that at my house, and if I'm in a car I don't play it, is the type of music that is about sex and so forth. Because I find that birth control pills and condoms and them things, it's teaching the children about sex. It's like you're pourin' some water in a basket, you understand what I'm saying? Old saying from long time in Jamaica is that prevention is better than cure. So instead of you try to cure the thing, you try to prevent it from happening. So why singin' about so much pussy and cocky and violence, and when the violence an' that come now, you can't run away from that. So if the music is promotin' violence or if the music is promotin' sex and them thing, I don't really like it, but I don't fight whosoever love it because everything have a season, and maybe some people love it, that's fine, but for me I don't check for that stuff.

Even sex and them thing, those should be a more secretive thing, secret thing, you know. Like you know some music that I see, some calypso music and some of those raw music about sex and thing, they should play that in clubs, where you have people over eighteen going to clubs or so on, and they windin' up to some naked music, and you have other music which is spiritual, which you can play anywhere, in any environment, anywhere anybody is, you know?

I'm not fightin' against nobody because everybody got to live, but if I got to live by the Devil way, I don't want to live that way. If I want to be happy and I gonna have some money and I gonna have a lot a things, just by leadin' the children astray and teachin' them some dirty things, then I don't want no money and I don't want to be big. And I don't want to promote no war against nobody, no color or no nation, because as a Rastaman, you know the Emperor Haile Selassie I, King of Kings, him have a speech that him made in Geneva, and that speech, I've got it framed in my house, him say, "Until the color of a man's skin is of no more significance than the color of his eyes, until there are no more first- and second-class citizens of any nation," I live with that in my heart and accept everyone as my brother. I can't cheat you and use you. Together we can make sweet music and we can make life nice and happy and achieve enough things that we want.

Singer-songwriter Ken Bob has been recording in Kingston studios for more than a decade.

Duckie Simpson (Black Uhuru)

The change [in reggae], really, it start from Selassie I death [1975], that is what the whole thing start from. Anyhow, from Bob Marley drop out, [Black Uhuru] came almost a year or two before Bob Marley drop out, get into the limelight, and when we came into the limelight, we had Culture, Burning Spear, Mighty Diamonds, which were really famous, and then we came into that world. Is like things deteriorate mentally after Bob died, after Selassie died, because then a lot of man lose the spirit and them confidence, a lot of guys trim [locks] and stuff. Then Bob died, now, and them say reggae dead, because the American them did only see Bob doing reggae, like Bob was the only artist, and Bob was the only Rasta.

Anyhow, the DJ shift the theme, the disc jockey them shift the music, you have a thing coming in now, the whole thing shift now, cocaine and drugs and the whole scene shift. The disc jockey them start playing different things, and you have a whole hypocritical element around the whole thing, because I seen people who is fighting down the music, they're the same ones who skinnin' out when they hear it. You go to all these uptown dances, they're skinnin' out, man, when you see them tomorrow they are, like, "Well, I don't like this"—bullshit, what they don't like about the dancehall music, all the small guys, these guys are like street guys, didn't have anything, and now they're driving Benz, and so it's more a grudge.

If the [police] commissioner arrest DJs for gun lyrics, that's their business, but I'm not against what's coming out . . . I'm not a fool . . . sex and gangsterism and violence, you don't have to buy it, you don't have to play it. But all these ladies in Jamaica, they love that kind of shit, you just go to parties and watch, they lift up their skirt when they hear it and show their panties. Carnival is the same thing. To tell the truth, reggae is getting more slacker than Carnival now, yeah, because these girls are showin' their private parts in reggae, when they dancin' reggae now. Carnival, they may be winin' up, but . . . I see girl dancin' and showin' their private parts, now, understand?

I don't care what anyone gonna say, I was the one who form this, build it, like on the radio in Boston, Michael Rose say that, like, Black Uhuru was street-corner singers until he make them into something . . . well, he's right, because I was a street-corner singer. Drifters was, Temptations was, and I don't feel no way about that, but when

BLACK UHURU (Don Carlos, Garth Dennis, Duckie Simpson)
Golden Spring, St. Andrew, 1992

he says he make us into what we were, that's lies, everybody knows where we come from, know the way we came up, they all know how we got to where we got to. So he's right in sayin' that we are street-corner singers—yeah, I'm a street-corner singer, I'm a street-corner guy, I'm proud of that.

This is how Uhuru came together—Garthie [Dennis] came into the neighborhood, I met Garthie, and after I met Garthie, we start talkin' about music, and formin' a group and stuff. Garthie told me that he know Bob Marley, I say, let's go check him out, so we start hangin' with Bob, Wailing Souls. I learned a lot from those guys, Pipe, Wailing Souls. This was about '72, '73. And I and Garthie was back and forth from Waterhouse to Trench Town every day for like eight years, every day, every single day, we spend like ten, twelve hours a day in Trench Town, rehearsin' along with Bob and Wailing Souls and learning the music, came back to Waterhouse.

You see, the whole thing, Black Uhuru, was like trick—Island [Records] trick us, right? The first album was for Jammy's, our second album was with Sly [Dunbar], that was the album that break us, and the next album was with Sly also, then we got signed to Island for Red. And Island had their lawyer there, and we didn't have a lawyer. We signed the contract, a one percent contract, and we got like $12,000 for the first contract, the next album was maybe $24,000, and up to this day I can't achieve no royalties, because they say I haven't finished payin'. I get $12,000 and one percent, but I owe these people.

Companies now signin' up all these new artists, and I'm sorry for them—I'm sorry for them. Like I've told my friends, man, you watch all these guys talking about getting big contract and big advance, best thing is work for a small company. Everybody want to sign to the big company, but fuck the big company. I want to sign with the small guy. And the only reason they're signing up all those DJs is to shelve them, like how they sign up all those rap artists and silence them. Because too much money was coming out of them, all these tycoons and their lawyers up there. All these DJs they sign, they can't even get a tour, the company can't put a tour together for them. Just sign them, give them some money, and quiet them.

Right now, Rasta take a backseat, it is not the time of creatin' or tryin' to show people what's going on; it's a time of war, you understand, so let the system do what it does, there's nothin' I&I can do.

Duckie Simpson is founder of Black Uhuru, whose former members have also included Junior Reid, Michael Rose, and the late Puma Jones.

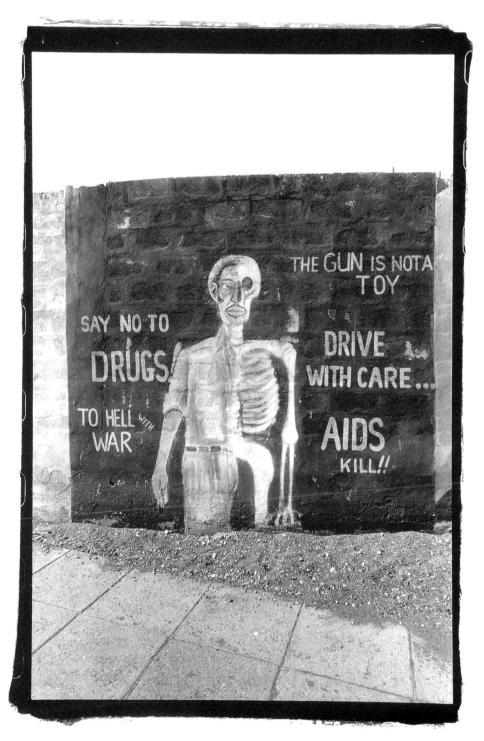

PUBLIC SERVICE ANNOUNCEMENT
Downtown Kingston

OKU ONUORA
"Like music, poetry is a universal language . . ."
West Kings House Road, Kingston

Oku Onuora

Reggae has gone a long way since its emergence, and you probably know a bit of the history, comin' from ska, rock steady, and then into reggae. Because of the richness of reggae, because of the heritage of reggae in that where it's coming from, and the influences, like African-derived rhythms like *mento, poco, kumina*, which gave rise to Rastafarian chants, drummin', which gave rise to ska and then to rock steady. Because of this rich cultural heritage of the music, it is able to shift—the colorin', we are able to vary the color. We have seen the dramatic development of the music since the mid-Eighties, where dancehall has taken over, it almost predominate the reggae arena. You see Shabba Ranks, for example, who got a Grammy—not that he was the first reggae artist to get a Grammy, but he's the first DJ. Because of the kind of publicity, the kind of deal, the kind of profile Shabba has received, we have never seen that before in the history of reggae. And it's surprisin' enough people in Europe, or other parts of the world, are fast gravitatin' towards the DJ music, the dancehall music.

What is unfortunate about the dancehall music is that the lyrical substance in most cases are not what is historically accepted or known about reggae. Reggae music is known as a protest music, it is known as a music which deals with the positive. There are some dancehall lyrics that tend to lean toward the cultural side, but not many. Most of the popular dancehall music are permeated with lyrics that one would consider "slack," for want of a better term.

I have nothing against the dancehall rhythm; I find it very hypnotic, very infectious, very danceable. In any music you have different degrees, different aspect of it, you have listenin' music, you have music where you relax by, and you have dancin' music. Now the dancehall music, as the name implies, is for the dance hall and not really something to listen to. It's really music for dancin', you know, it's dancehall music, music for dancin'. For awhile I was a bit concerned, and still concerned to a degree, because there wasn't anything innovative happenin' in the music. More recently, we have seen some kinda innovation, we're getting all these stripped-down basic rhythms that on the surface appear quite simple. So we see some kinda freshness happenin', and this was absent for awhile. It's gettin' more interestin'.

It's also forcin' a lotta people, reggae artists of the Sixties, Seventies, to actually re-evaluate their musical presentation, not just the instrumentation but also the presentation. Because the dancehall artists, you know, come about with this kind of flamboyant image thing. And then, probably one of the reason or one of the factor which assisted the dancehall artists to become popular, or in thing, is because of the image, and today people are more attracted to audio-visual images, you know, we live in a age where audio-visual presentation plays an important role.

So, in a way, the transition in the music, or the change that has taken place, has its positive and its negative sides to it. I've already mentioned the negative side, where dancehall music seems to be flooded with slack, lewd lyrics, with a certain kinda crudity in its presentation, too. But then the crudity is also part of the make-up and the reality from which it comes, from which that particular aspect of the music comes.

What the dancehall music has done, the present state of the dancehall music, it has opened more doors. It has created space for the growth of the music entirely. For the first time we are seeing more than one major company signing reggae acts. Prior to now, we just had a handful, but now find like major independent labels are signing reggae acts. At the moment, you have several reggae acts signed to major labels, and the interest in the music is growing. So this is one of the positive aspects about it. Whether the people in the Jamaican music industry will take cue from the major companies that are handling the acts that are now signed to them, and actually upgrade their approach, refine the mannerism, and utilize organizational methods of dealing with the business, that is left to be seen. You know like with fashion, music is the same thing. Styles change. A new wave of music, everybody want to be first or everybody want to maximize, everybody want to get as much outta it, and the same thing is happening to reggae at the moment. It's happened—we saw the lambada dance come, we saw break dance come, we see even with rap, the attention that rap used to get four years ago, it is not actually getting now. As to how long this present enthusiasm about the dancehall music and DJ will last, is yet to be seen. I not attempt to make any kind of predictions at all. All I'd like to say is that, given the present climate at the moment, where recording companies who would not even give a split second to reggae music, they are now paying attention to reggae music, and this can only be beneficial to the industry as a whole, and to the music in general.

At the same time, the cultural aspect of the music, which for a time appeared dead, seem to be becomin' alive once more, and this is probably because of the climate of the world today. You find that people are faced with some serious problems, inflation, disease, housing, wars, 'cause right now we see all over Europe there's civil strife, in the Middle East, in Africa. And people, although they need to escape, or a lot of people try to escape from the reality, because of the harshness of the realities that we are facin' now, you know, them have to really deal with it. So therefore it seems as if once again the cultural aspect of the music is slowly becomin' alive once again.

Dub poetry have not received the kind of attention that it ought to have received. We have made great strides, I mean, the poets have made great strides, the poets have a audience, they have fared very well over the years. In fact, they have made some serious impact in areas where, you know, dancehall artists or singers have not done. It's not a popular form as yet, and the potential for it to become a popular form is still there, because of the opportunity of the poets, the dub poets, to be versatile, because of the universal acceptability of poetry. Like music, poetry is a universal language. Within every culture, one can identify the poetry, even if the rhythm is different, even if it's a different style of poetry. Poetry as a art form is the oldest, and this gives it a certain kind of credibility.

POET AND PERFORMANCE ARTIST JEAN BREEZE

WATERFALL ALONG CANE RIVER
St. Andrew

I feel probably people have not given the time to seriously deal with the form. Nobody has ever tried to market it seriously, no one. Even with Linton Kwesi Johnson on Island Records, no recordin' company to date have decided to deal with this. But then, unlike ten years ago, unlike five years ago, poetry, the dub poetry has become more prolific. You find people in South Africa, we have people from other parts of Africa, we have people in Germany, in Canada, in the U.S., in the U.K., who are practicin' dub poets, both male and female. And a few of them succeeded to a degree in what they are doing. It's just a matter of time and hard work.

What is happenin' also, because DJ music is presented in the spoken word form, you know, it's poetry, it's poetry. So therefore with the popularity of the dancehall music and particularly deejaying, it also helps to facilitate the wider acceptance of dub poetry. About dub poetry I can say I see in the near future dub poetry going to be a serious musical form. People will have to pay attention to it, things will be happenin' in that arena. It has not been exploited . . . it's still fresh, and because of that freshness, the possibility are there.

One of Jamaica's most widely published poets, Oku Onuora is a pioneer of dub poetry. His stage performances with live reggae bands are not to be missed.

Yasus Afari

Man and his total experience give rise to language. Language is meant to communicate man's thoughts and experiences and aspirations. Music happen to be a manifestation of the soul, the soul language, so what happen in the mind of the people and the mind of the nation must be reflected in artistic and other expression. So we would say now, is what the DJs are expressing is a reflection of the nation—at the same time, what the DJ a do help shape what take place in the nation. So there is a parallel between violence in the music and violence in the society. Therefore, you have a great sense of responsibility to create that delicate balance, so that we can accommodate artistic expression, which reflect what go on in the nation, but to have that sense of responsibility and direction and moral goodness. So actually the influence should be a corrective measure—to improve and not to deteriorate further.

Language goes all over the world, so everyone is a poet in that sense. The essence of language or communication is in the poetry state, the arrangement of your talk. Now in terms of professional poetry, like in our case, we are an artist or so-called dub poet, even though still it all depend on how you define dub poetry. We define it as being the process of extracting negativity and injecting positivity through our form of poetry—words, sounds—is like, in that sense now, in our sense, a liberation tool. So is in that sense you call a person a dub poet. With the advent of dub poetry, and inroads made into the dance hall, dub poetry have overwhelmed the whole thing, too. 'Cause if you realize, we a now a claim every man now and make a man say a poem. Inevitably you are a poet, you can't escape. Once you are a poet, you get to be a dub poet—go extract negativity and inject positivity. So, that are the future and it a happen. We can offer an alternative to society.

That's why me personally, any man who define himself as an artist and a messenger, we have a responsibility to help monitor and exert influence, make sure, say, it is in the interest of the nation, is in the interest of the people. So that is what music is all about, it is communication with your Creator, your whole environment. Music is really a sacred, divine thing, which is a form of medicine, a form of giving praise, a form of weapon, is a love thing, is an emotional, sexual, charming thing. So we say, since we create an indigenous art form, our music, we should evolve it to a level where it benefit humanity, and is honorable in the eyes of the Creator. That's what I&I are about, you know.

In terms of that now, we realize that we are a country with laws. We have a lot of DJ now who are anti-government, anti-establishment, them see certain things what happen, and maybe them not satisfied with how the police deal with it, or how the establishment deal with it, so [it] is a form of energy and them give it off. The so-called leaders are people who shape and influence the society, must take up responsibility now to try channel that energy and be creative, not destroy. They can change from one form to the next. Channel that energy, even destructive energy, toward the proper things.

So, make that music the conscience of the nation, and influence parents, teachers, leaders, authors, whoever have an influence, journalists, disk jockeys, managers or producers or promoters. Look 'pon the songs that they sing over now, the songs done a long time ago, you know. Suppose them songs deal with wickedness and destruction . . . now, in ten years time, the pickney start to sing them over, is a thing that repeat destruction. So them must be careful of what them doing. You look at it that way, and you meditate 'pon it, because, is a seed you sow, and is a crop you plant, and you must not plant poisonous plant or the youth is going to get it.

Rastafari is the only authentic and indigenous response to colonialism and imperialism and slavery. Therefore, Haile Selassie come out of Ethiopia to teach the family of humanity, the new Africa and Ethiopia and new world order, which is honor, which is referenced by the human soul. So, humans is a family under the sun and the moon and the stars. Why they no answer that? Why do religions not teach that? Where does the illusion or fantasy come? Reality is eternity. That makes you work on your music or your expression—the original order, the foundation or the natural order, the Creator order. That's what my music is all about.

Me no shove nothin' down no man throat, and no guy shove nothin' down my throat either. You supposed to influence as well as be influenced, it all depends on your strength of character, and strength of persuasion, and sense of purpose, and dignity, and integrity, and humanity. Me no have a problem, because right now, all my meditation is for a better human race, and a better spirit, an instrument of the almighty Creator.

Yasus Afari's unique blend of dub poetry and dancehall riddims is showcased on his debut album, Dancehall Baptism, *on RAS Records.*

MUTABARUKA AT "BOOKS ABOUT US"
New Kingston

BOB MARLEY MURAL, WEST KINGSTON
Trench Town

MICHAEL ROSE
"Nothing is better than acoustic . . ."
Kingston, May 1992

Michael Rose

As the music goes along, you must try an improvement, because if the music doesn't have improvement, it will get tiring to the public, so you just have to accept these changes, you know. It's just a different taste, you know, because if you notice, everybody does [computer] programming today. But nothing is better than acoustic, you understand, it comes right back to acoustic, so is just like you can't run away from reggae, you can't run away from acoustic.

Most of the youth them that comin' up right now, you see it's like they have not thought of the reality side of what is happening in the world. Yeah? 'Cause most a them is like, it's just lovers' rock. Is music all over, but is just like, you know, certain people can do certain work and some people just can't. This is why people like Ziggy Marley, Michael Rose, Burning Spear, have to come presently right now to make certain sounds be heard, because people are there waiting. Is not everybody really can take the lovey lovey. Because you know about love, is understood, if you can't sing something about what is happening in the world today, to help the kids them so they don't go wrong. Lovers' rock, nothing is wrong with it, but you just have to have the messengers there to take the message on a level, so it reach nations, because if it don't reach nations, it can be very dangerous. Like what happen in the world today.

Japanese people, they are just catching on fully to reggae. They love Bob Marley. Bob Marley is a messenger-singer, and like some people who like Bob Marley don't really check to like lovey-dovey songs, so you still have to have sugar and milk, is not only milk alone sweeten coffee, and is not sugar alone. You still have to have the two, but you have to balance, you just have to balance.

From ever since, European people love reggae, 'cause it's just like Bob Marley never have a hit song, but he's sold copies like cookie, so it's like Europe did ready long time, America and the rest of the world, they get hip to it now, which is good. Disco music come from reggae, from the reggae drum and bass, this is how the Americans invent disco, from long time. And now them move on to another stage them call hip-hop. Long time ago, you used to have the black Americans, they would say, like, "I'm an American," they never into reggae. Is just that of recent, what we've been trying to show them over the years has become a reality presently today. So is like, a lot a them is catchin' on, and tryin' to pick up, a lot a them doing a lot of researches right now from what they've been slippin' upon.

To tell you the truth, it's the new age kids, it's the kids that they are bornin' now, like the younger ones, because the elder ones, they didn't wanna hear nothin' about reggae. The younger ones are the ones that are interested in repatriation and all this, they know that they have to go home to Africa, because the West must perish. With all that gwan the West must perish, believe me, man. The struggle that you see goin' on in Africa, with all those people dyin' and all those things, the West will be like that, because they stole all the resources like grain, gold, diamond, everything that's supposed to keep the people them well fed, they bring everything in the West to survive the West. So if them do that, you must expect people to a suffer. There's nothing left. Because them can't see it, they don't know whatever happen, so it's either them free up from now or it's gonna be terrible, man. America, them a look for a new enemy, because the people in the West they like war, you know. West people are gunslingers, man.

You know, is like, reggae is just like Africa. Africa is the foodbasket for the world, reggae will be the foodbasket for the world, feed the people spiritually. Yeah man, Rastafari know that I&I Father is not around, nobody can see him. You have a lot a propaganda goin' around about, they want people to rectify this, that, that, that. And in earlier time nobody interested, so how come they're interested today? What these guys are tryin' to prove? A lot a things is gonna happen, man, 'cause these people, they never learn. They've been taught and they don't wanna listen, and then when it's too late, they wanna listen, and it's already too late. You have to learn by your mistakes.

Michael Rose's unique voice and musical arrangements have been heard on record since the Seventies.

DINNER HOUR
Snake Hill, St. Catherine

CULTURE ON STAGE
Foreground: Joseph Hill
Background: Albert Walker, Kenneth Dayes

Joseph Hill

A lot of people, you cannot even leave a message with them. You got to let what's happening to them give them a message, then you don't control it. What's happening to them give them a message. For instance, what's happening here in Jamaica. We kept giving Jamaica messages, people like myself, Burning Spear, we don't have to give Jamaica another message, you know, because they have already heard, they have been warned. Right? They have been warned. How many people warn them? Brother Bob warn them, "Stiff-necked fool, you think you are cool, to deny me for simplicity." Yes, they deny the world on behalf of politics, now politics is pouring out its corruption.

I think that they should set their cups and drink, because that's what they want. Because, you know, in my opinion, all Jamaica needs is for everybody to put their head together and just do some strong farmin'! Stop the talking! I don't have any word to give anybody. If I have a machete and you need one, you can get it. Talk is cheap. Very, very, very cheap—doesn't take any gas. Needs no transport and no visa. Nothing looks after it and it looks after nothing. That's for talk.

So many people, peace is not their life, war is their life. They make money off of war and spend money on peace, is that not so? But they don't even spend any money for peace—you know, not for my peace. And peace don't even have to be made. Right now, here we are, you don't even hear a vehicle, maybe the sound of reggae in the background, our speech. What more peacefulness can a person need? I hear everybody keep talking, "Come down to town, go downtown." I want anything to buy in town, I'm going. There is perfect innocence here where we are, and there is war downtown. I believe, if the war continue forever, then Jah would be sleeping. You know what I mean? Rasta!

I man supposed to try all the wise country. Born in this country, live here, my history is between here and the rest of the world, wherever I go. No two-page book, write history that everybody can see, and even if today the war should reach right here and they should shoot me off this chair, this is my last word: we need peace, war still can't resolve the problem. 'Cause I man see many wars, and the problem still remain. You can see clearly for yourself that war cannot solve the problem. Peace does not come out of a gun, I'm

JOSEPH HILL
"I've got a Bible. You keep the gun . . ."
Mannings Hill

sure. It's too bad they don't make any peace bullet. And they don't make any refrigerator to preserve life. Right now they're talking about war on the radio—I switch it off. I don't pay light bill to listen to that! Stupidness!

Look at it, look how far in this mountain I live. And you know, politician have the heart to come all the way down in this place and tell me to come out on the street and go and vote. I say what for? I'm not depending on the government for my living. I'm not concerned about that. I'm concerned about getting 25 acres of land, that I can plant surplus food to feed somebody else. Politician, he's not talking to me about that. He's talking about votes and guns. I don't need a gun, 'cause you don't need a gun to praise Jah. I've got a Bible inside my house, that's it. You keep the gun.

(Mannings Hill, February 1992)

The most we can talk about is what life have taught us. That's my topic, what life have taught me. Well, in my time, I have seen the typewriter, which is of use to me, the telephone, the camera, the tape machine, the recording studio, the buses and trucks, the cars, even a bicycle, even a pair of shoes, a pair of socks, clothing, is of use to all of us. In the particular title track called "Good Things," well, I am referring to all of them.

The presidents all over the world, the prime ministers, and the assisting ministers and bodies should take a deep look in, is to see that the biggest commodity on earth is man, mankind. There ain't nothing more valuable. So then, man in return make all these equipment, and at the same time, some of them are not making good use of them. So then I, Joseph Hill, in return, just trying to remind everybody, "Make good use of good things while it comes your way/Make good use of the good things while they still love you." Because if you are being a monument of hate, or a monument of hatred in this world, then your value is worth nothing, right?

But with love, the whole world is unlimited. With love, life is worthwhile living. With love, we know the value of each other. With love, there ain't no use for a condom. With love, there ain't no use for abortion. With love, the guns could be abolished. With love, snow would go away and leave a tropical climate all over the world, and food continually would come from under the earth. With love and without contamination, we could live forever.

Massive to massive is not making any war. Government to government makes war. The people don't want to fight—so why don't the government get out and fight? Go on out! The innocent brothers don't need to go to Vietnam. They don't need to go to Falklands. They don't need to go to Grenada. They don't need to go to Panama or anywhere. The rich man sends his money through the pockets of the poor—to war! And the rich man sits down in corrupted luxurious peace.

Well, my term about peace is, I don't want no peace. Because I don't know how big the piece is that I shall get. I want a half, which is equal rights and justice. A half between us, there can't be an injustice there. But, you know what could be the tactics in a peace: "Oh, Tom want a piece," he gets a little scrap, the crumb. Yes? If the fly pitch over the crumb, the fly is bigger than the crumb. I don't want no piece! Give me half! Don't give me no piece, give me half. Because a half to me appears to be equal rights and justice. Somebody wants a piece one inch thick by a inch wide. The other person wants a piece six inches wide by twelve inches thick by a mile long. It is named the same piece. It's a piece of it. You get a piece of the action. Just a piece of the action. And for that piece of the action, for the rest of your life, you suffer loss. The nation suffers loss. Yeh? The children suffer loss. They didn't get too much a big piece of the schooling. They end up being a dunce. That's not equal rights and justice, that's just peace. The peace that they are talking about is for you to fold your hands, shut your mouth at every condition. No way!

When you ask about real peace, real love, international togetherness, when you talk about universal quietness, even though that cannot be had, even then, at the same time, there can be some encouragement towards it. But there are people who still don't want that. All they want is, like, all for themselves. In fact, the world today, it is only showing me "no get" for the needy and all for the greedy. No get, which mean the needy ain't getting any, and all belongs to the greedy. No get for the needy and all for the greedy. All of self, none of thee. Things like that should be abolished long, long, long, long centuries ago.

(Cleveland, U.S.A., January 1990)

One of the hardest-working people in reggae, Joseph Hill is the leader of the roots trio Culture. They have released more than a dozen albums on Jamaican and international labels since the early Seventies. He is proprietor of the Channel 7 sound system.

HELLSHIRE BEACH

"DADDY" U ROY
"You don't have to have a million dollar to give your bredrin a dollar . . ."
New York, 1994

"Daddy" U Roy

I feel good about everything that's going on, because, I mean, reggae music is on the upward right now, it's kind of steppin' up now, you know, comparing to some years ago. I like some of the recent DJs, you know, because for me as one of the original conscious DJs, I like the conscious type of lyrics. Any DJ talkin' consciousness, I love that. The same thing with singers, I love every singer singin' the conscious stuff.

People kind of be realizing, hey, everybody hear about under this lady's dress, and they hear about how big your gun is, and who you supposed to smoke out from who not to get smoke out. The people hear a lot of this, and now they want to get back to some more cultural singers. And also, the singers and the DJs and rappers and whatever you call them, is like, everybody kind of teaching, I wouldn't say everybody, but most people are teaching conscious right now, you know, and I like that.

You see, youth is one of the main supporters of the music, these young little kids, and, is like whatever their favorite singer or DJ say to them, that's what they take onto, you know? You know what I mean? And also, like, some of the DJs and singers, you can't even blame them for what they are doing, 'cause it's the quickest way to make some money for them right now, it's even better than going and putting a gun in somebody's face and take their purse, or stuff like that. The DJs kind of pushing that. I think what's gonna have to happen is that, everyone gwan to just realize that, hey, this is wrong, so let's change this. The rappers and the DJs and singers that are talkin' slack stuff, is like, after a while that just don't really make much sense. Everything they talk about ladies is kind of disrespectful to my mother and my sister. And then some of these DJs, they feel bad about it, but they just can't afford to show they feel bad; they just take it for a laugh and make it look like they did say something good. That's just the way it is.

As I say before, guys are talking consciousness, I like them, you know. For me, hip-hop, that rap stuff, is just another form of [reggae] DJ, this is the American form, you know. This is just the American form of DJ, man, and whenever we go and check it, is the same thing I man used to do when I start, you have the singer sing, and you come in and DJ, same thing when the rappers, they have the singers come in and sing some nice things, and them DJ. Is just the same thing. All I have to say about this is just, we just want some conscious lyrics, you know, something that, you don't have to hear your Mom comin' and turn the tape off, or your parents listen and say, "Hey, don't play that tape inside here!" You know what I mean?

I think the Japanese people, I don't know, but I think these people study [reggae] to the heights and depths, and I see them and wonder how in the world these people know these things. But, you know, is like when they interested in somethin' it's just like they put their heads to it. I can tell you, I hear a ska band in Japan, and this is a all-Japanese ska band we're talkin' about here now, and, hey, if you lock them into a room, you don't know if Roland Alphonso and Tommy McCook is in there or not. If you lock them into a room and go say who played, you would say, Tommy McCook and Roland Alphonso and all the Skatalites is in this room. When you open that door, you'd be surprised! You know? Because these people, I think these people take the music quite serious and quite deep.

In Japan, they know the man who start this thing, they know your music that you start recording with, and they know your current [records]. And I tell you, a lot of people all over still like that. Like, I've been to Holland, and met this young college kid, this kid is like about 22 years old, and I'm talkin' like I'm thirty years older than this kid, and he can tell me every song that I put out, some that I don't even remember, and this is a kid that is 22 years old going to college.

Look, these people are so . . . they love a lot of other cultures, a lot of music—believe me, don't think it's reggae alone—the people, OK, Japan, when you go to Japan, you see posters put up of all different rap groups and all different singin' groups, and you see the same thing even in France, where you see singers like Janet Jackson. A lot of singers go there and they sold out 100 percent, even more than reggae, but there is people that are just, they're into the music, it's like music is their life, and if they're hearing some good music, man, everything is cool for them. Is like me, sometimes I will have some problem, and if I hear true good music, it can pick me up and the problems kind of fly away for the time being.

Well, I tell you something, is only one thing I can say right now, it's judgment time. This tribulation is like . . . everything, everybody is at war right now, everywhere you go is war, war, war. I think that something is really wrong, but I don't know . . . I mean, you always have these little gangster wars and everything like that, guys warrin' about their girl, and this guy say, he's tougher than that guy.

You know, these are things that go on everywhere and every time, you know, it's just that these people need to get more conscious, need to find somethin' to do, you know. Some of these people that have been doin' some of these stupid wars, they don't have nothin' to do, they just being idle, sitting down, don't have nothin' to do, OK, let's raise hell now.

The people that have something to think about, they have a kid, they think about how the hell is my kid going to eat, how am I going to eat, how is my woman going to eat, how is my house gonna run, then you wouldn't have the time for war. You see? A lot of these people that are doing these [violent] things, hey, they don't have nothin' else to do. I don't think all these little stupid wars, and tribal wars, and things like this are new . . . it's been goin' on since creation, like since the beginning of this world, and it still continue. Some people, they just want to war. Some people is just people who want war, and the only thing they love more than war is more war.

You don't have to have a million dollar to give your bredrin a dollar, or give your bredrin a five dollar. You can just have twenty dollars and you give a man two dollars and you still have eighteen, and he's gonna get some food to eat or something. As a youth, you know, I used to play a sound [system] and work on construction site. One day, I go out from the construction site, for my lunch, you know, and when I go out to get my lunch and come back, ready to eat, and I see this one guy, and I say to him, "Hey, how come you're not eatin'?" And he say to me, "Well, I just start this mornin', you know, and I'm not gonna get paid for two weeks' time." I cut my lunch in half and I give him half. I don't know why I am doing this, it must be the Most High tellin' me to do it. And I see another man, and say to him, "How come you're not eatin'?" and him say, "I just start yesterday, you know, and I don't get paid for two weeks' time." And I cut my half in half and I give this man half of my half, and believe me, I eat my quarter, and is like, for the rest of the day, is like some burden come off of my head, is like some pressure come off of me. I feel like I want to fly! I go to my bed and I start dreamin' that I'm flyin', for like three or four weeks. And believe me, I'm flyin' all over the place now.

"Daddy" U Roy, one of the most beloved figures in reggae, was interviewed by phone from his home in California. He plans to get his sound system back in operation in Jamaica soon.

HALF PINT
"*From out of ignorance, anger, and crime, you will still find mercy . . .*"
Manor Park, St. Andrew

Half Pint

All I can explain is that everybody is more like rushin' in a race, livin' in the fast lane, go get it, go get it, and nobody really watchin' their step or trying to pace themself, brace themself, tryin' to keep them balance. Them overdo it, some gone as far as constant wantin' to be on the charts, constant wantin' to be like the famous one, and in spite of that them lyrics is not totally put together, sometimes songs has been contradictin' other songs, because of the ego. Everybody tryin' to see themself more like the frontrunner, or themself to be like on the front line. And then at the same time, everybody can't be there at the same time, so it actually been a confusion and a disturbed way about the whole industry, because when the artist in person start to be like that, the whole industry falls into that same category.

Even the distributin' companies now get that attitude, to be like, keep pushin' out, pushin' out all different artists. The next thing is that each artist don't realize how the whole thing is goin'. The producers for one tend to be like producin' songs which maybe become a hit, then they find about ten more artists to be on that same riddim, and then currently you find that one riddim lasts about three month, and whenever that riddim finish, all the artists who were on that riddim, it's like, they gone again. And by them rushin' on next riddim again what they might think is on the horizon, their lyrics are not ready, not set. So those are the area me see which more disturb the music.

Sooner or later, if it don't happen naturally to bring a more relaxation within the music, I figure it will happen in a more destructive way, before one can realize or start a build up again. Because the foundation set already, and people now is like passin' the brick, and still put in some of the brick with less mortar. . . . Some of the artist them a figure if they did respect themselves and what they are sayin' and what they are doin', and know what they are goin' into, they would be more cautious and more presentin' lyrics which don't react back on them or contradict them own lifestyle, use lyrics which at times even cost them own life.

They messin' up the youth, man, because, no man never born big. Me no find them that real, them not thinkin' for themself really, neither. Them lyrics not come from them heart. Them just like feel like them want to sing, them just want to be on the stage, them just want to be in the limelight or the spotlight. Give the people what they want—that's bull, right. Give them what them need, not what them want, what them need is the real stuff which tell them how life goes, this is this and that is that, because no man never born big. All kinda lyrics what tell people 'bout kill, kill, and shot and shot and shot, I mean, you have some people who can be easily led, and you have some people who strong enough, but sometime too, some people who keep pushin' it, pushin' it, pushin' it, tellin' them, tellin' them, is just like temptation. And all these lyrics that tell about kill, kill, murder, is like them a paint a picture, a bloody scenery, in other people them mind.

Me no really condemn them or judge them, is only who did strong enough to play with the fire and never get burned? Some people love to exercise themselves that way until you say, they livin' out their fantasy. But fantasies sometimes turn out to be illusions, and if you live by illusion, if you no strong enough, it take you over and make you deal with destruction come. If you preachin' it, why you not thinkin' of preachin' or exercisin' something inna more good, more than the gun who kill. Don't make it sound like you boost it or push it down on some a the younger youths. The younger youths them come now who are not intelligent enough, they will take it on more faster mentally than how a bigger or older person would, seen? The kids them take it on more faster. The kids don't know, them more hot-blooded.

The reality of life is what I feel outside, with the breeze, the stars, nighttime, or whatever, that is what "hardcore" really mean. Raggamuffin, a youth who grow up outside where him can stand the weather and no havin' the flu, him can stand hunger, him can stand a pain, him can endure. A lot a people interpret raggamuffin as if it a criminal morality. What I mean, even the movie, *Oliver Twist*, it was when raggamuffin come about, him remember even Oliver Twist is a kid who born a certain way and because of circumstances. Jesus Christ himself, in a stable him born, him a king. Some guy a tell you, I wanna be rich, I want a satellite dish, and them tell you it's reality, and by getting that reality them hurt a lot more people. Them doing themselves a favor, they live the best, but they do the worst to the people before them, them disturb many other people mind.

Me know that today, stress, poverty, and the pain of the world, it breeds crime, ignorance, and anger. But from out of ignorance, anger, and crime you still find mercy, and even if you have one little root of mercy in it, it will grow and blossom. So that's where I find my inspiration in it still.

Half Pint released his first single, "Sally," in 1981. He has been recording and performing worldwide ever since.

Plesant day to The Honourable
almighty god, Emancipation,
Proclaima Tion, 2nd, of, aug year, to
year, the, Time has come For
The Police to Watch the, Jamaican
aFrican, People Home, god the
almighty going To Reveal
himSELF Through Culley
gong-gonga Rao.G. maragh
maragh
PLesAnT day to
all The JaMaIcan
AFrican, PeoPLe We are
A Pair of Prisoner LIKE
Brother manDella
and sister, Mandella
Brother Levine
Sister Levine, Mr L.P.H.

WATER HOUSE CREW (MASSOP, TEX, AND KIRK)

SUGAR BLACK (HOLDING GUITAR) AND LEHBANCHULEH
Kingston

WRITING ON THE WALL
Water House

JUNIOR REID
"Reggae is aimin' to the highest level . . ."

Junior Reid

I know that for reggae music through the Nineties and all times, you know, in the future, it's gonna be real massive, it's gonna be the next thing, upside all the pop songs and all those songs worldwide.

Reggae music is big big big in Europe right now, Japan, America, Africa, and there still people out there in the world, they're still lookin' forward to the consciousness of the music. Musical arrangement and changes in it, not the one-chord things, you know. The Japanese them not so fast like the Americans. They more easy backin' like Jamaica, so they easier to communicate, 'cause Americans are fast onto you. Busy and so-so.

American audiences are tough. With rap now, reggae it catchin' on. The original rap beat come from the reggae beat, and right now the reggae beat is just kinda comin' up front, 'cause all the other beat get borin', you know? So even Michael Jackson have to come now on the reggae beat, all a them have to come on the reggae beat.

Time ago you used to have DJs, Big Youth who come in singin' and deejayin', but now they bring it back around in modern style, computer beat, and mix female singers and DJ, or male singers and DJs, and it appealing to people.

I work with DJ still, and do combination, but I more concentratin' on straight consciousness. When you do the other way, pop type, is a shortcut, y'understand? It don't show the true you, and you have to go and tour in a package with whosoever you work with, it's not like you're doing something your own, like your own show. Even if you try to do it, it don't sound as real as it sound on the record, or maybe they get somebody out there to full in that gap, and if him a DJ, him pick up a spot, or if he's a singer, he sing a spot, get a guy to come in and toast or sing. I think it help it 'cause it open up ways for the music still.

Where I see reggae goin' now, reggae is aimin' to the highest level, 'cause we as reggae singer do a lot a hard work and we make a lot a sacrifice to really goin' on forward. Man like Bob Marley, Peter Tosh, Hugh Mundell, all a them contribute in turn, but right now I don't see it goin' to a waste. I can see bright light for reggae music. Long time ago, it didn't have the strength, now it have big strength for the business, so is more force, you know?

Recent releases by the always prolific Junior Reid include Listen to the Voices *and* Crime Monster. *He was interviewed at his Kingston studio, JR Music.*

EDI FITZROY
"Respect the music and love the music . . ."
Kingston, 1993

Edi Fitzroy

Reggae right now, it have grown from one level to another, right, because, like, ten years ago, you had mostly the old Niyabinghi chant, which is roots rock. Well, it have changed so dramatically because of the whole, say, drum machine, you find say you don't really hear the acoustic sound anymore, and is like a new sound, you know, and especially like most a the young generation now, they're more hip on this sound. But what I get to find out is that the acoustic sound, which is the orthodox—we a call it reggae in the sense of true reggae—I found it still, OK like in Europe and those places, right. I found out that the whole hip-hop sound is most liked in America and the West Indies and place like those, but reggae within its true rights—people like Burning Spear, people like Jimmy Cliff, just thinking the roots-rock-reggae sound, I think it is more appreciated internationally than the drum machine, which is just like the fast beat, you know.

I think that there's nothing wrong with [computer riddims], you know, but I think usin' the original sound I feel is better, you know, it have more depth, it have more life in it. Because I listen to an album done by this drum machine . . . it's slightly empty, there's no feeling there, because, as one might say, it's really coming from a human being playing from the heart, you know. There's nothing there, you know. For me as an artist, personally speaking, I personally like the acoustic sound, which is go in the studio and lay the tracks with your drummer and your bass player and, you know, support, percussionists.

To me, it's like a cash-in program, like the [record] companies see where them can cash in and make some money now, you see, it's not really a long-term, like building an artist, you know, for a long-term project, is like they just get some quick money. And that is, I don't think . . . and I don't think that's really doing really good for the music on the whole, because if something's not goin' to last, they cannot be doing something good, you understand what I mean? You just take an artist and nurture that artist and build that artist, like how Island took Bob Marley and build him and, you know, today that legacy is still there, you know, is the foundation of the whole reggae vibes, you know, 'cause reggae is Bob, you know.

You can take anything and once you promote it, it must sell. Because the few [songs] pumped on the radio station every day, R&B songs, and the people hear reggae less, calypso less, rock less, then them are just going to go for what them hear more. You know, you totally brainwash them in what you play more, and right now rap music play more in Jamaica than singing, or even in America now, rap music play among black audience and white audience. Like Snow, I mean, they just take him and turn him into a mega-star overnight, and, what? He's not really singing, or singing about some of his realities, he's just singing about . . . the dance hall, so, let's just see how long it can last then, you know. Because I know that it have to come back to the real thing, and it is still, they say it have to come back to the real thing because the riddim that they are using in the dance hall is the real thing, it is the authentic hardcore reggae rock from the Sixties.

You must see that it is politics, I guess [politicians] don't want people really open to certain kinds of things, because of certain po-litical reasons, because if the people are fooled, then things are much easier, who are governing and who are ruling, because the people aren't . . . open to certain things, and there are people who will sit and take stupidness, you know what I mean, so . . . just make them lose them way within folly grounds and sex and . . . you know . . . I mean all the songs that are sex, sex, sex, sex, sex, sex, are just a joke—there's nothing wrong about sex, and sex is fun, and sex is spiritual, and sex is emotion, but it can't be too much of sex or peo-ple get bored. It just becomes monotonous, too much of a thing is not good. Most definitely.

What I would like to say right now, I personally as an artist still . . . just paint it right within the people's mind, you know, to really tell them things, what is really happening, the realistic sense of life, seen? 'Cause I don't really believe in fantasy and illusion—I'm not really a dreamer nor a schemer, you know, I have to just tell it like it is still, I'm not one person that really hide from any-thing. You know? As Bob Marley say, you can fool the people sometime, but you can't fool them all the time. Because music is one of the greatest educational platform within the society, you know, that's what teaches the people. And that's why it can put the people under. I just feel that there is a total campaign right now to put the people under, why they're pushing sex within the whole music, and divert the whole thing from the eye-opener to just style and fashion and dressin' and just dancehall wear and junk, and everything just break away and wind up and bend down and touch you toes, you know what I mean? And tomorrow, man, they wake up to the real issue.

SINGER/SONGWRITER BERES HAMMOND

[DJs say] it's slackness the people them want . . . no, not slackness the people them want, people don't want nothing dirty and derogative, but is what them feed the people with, it's what you give them. So there's no true value, there's no true sense of value right now. A guy have his last ten dollar, and go buy a pair of shoes with the ten dollar. You no see it? And then tomorrow, man, him dead fi hungry. He no know them priority. He could buy a pair of shoes for two dollar, save back eight dollar. But now everyone must want to try to impress another man, because everything has become materialistic minded. So you just have more robbery, people lose them sanity, 'cause people do anything to wear the latest style. But they're not gonna do anything to really get an education, have a family value, and teach a family what to choose or what not to choose. So the world is facing a serious problem, and the music can bring it back around. You no see?

I just keep doing what I'm doing, because I know that what I'm doing is right, because twenty years from now I know I'll be on stage, singing what I've been singing from 1980. People have been playing Bob Marley from the Sixties, just hearing a Bob song now from the Seventies, it's like it was yesterday it was recorded. Fresh. Because Bob him tell the people something. It's not fantasizing or an illusion or them things. People listen to the Beatles, it's the same way, John Lennon was one of those guys, because them guys really tell you certain things. They have a message. Stevie Wonder. 'Cause music have no barriers.

I feel that roots rock reggae is much more big-up, it have a bigger scope in the universe. More power to them artists still who just open the doors with it. You can't get pent up in just one thing, you have to explore. What really move the crowd, is you say the right thing. Just say the right thing. If you really tell them how to live, somebody care for them, you must love the daughter, love the country, love the music, respect people. Respect the music and love the music. Dancehall is the next trend, but keep it clean, because it can teach the future. Don't tell the teenager just about gun and sex . . . build their mind . . . love your brother, stop the shooting, end the war. Peace!

Singer Edi Fitzroy has been performing in Jamaica and abroad for more than fifteen years. His most recent album, Deep in Mi Culture, *is on the Henry K label. He is currently working on his next release.*

Ken Boothe

First person who actually put out my voice on the recording form is Duke Reid. But was a duo, not solo singing, it was a duo with Stranger Cole. And we did a couple a songs, I think he release one, Duke Reid. So we sing on corners, like in America, guys singin' on the corner, and, well, Sir Coxsone [Dodd], now, heard about us, songs on Duke Reid, people start talk about us, Sir Coxsone heard about us and send for us. So we did the first recording with him, a soft music, kinda American thing, the title of it was "My Marie," and he thought that we had those capabilities, those kinda sound, he didn't want to test us in ska. 'Cause we come at the last part of ska, you know. Me and Stranger Cole did "Marie," and then we did a ska tune, now, "World's Fair," and that came out and did quite well.

And Sir Coxsone call me on in his office, and said he think I should start singin' solo, 'cause he told me he never hear anything like me. He said he never hear no voice like mine. But I didn't realize that I could sing solo, I didn't think I was that good, you know. Sir Coxsone encourage me, and told me, just keep going in the studio, alone, whenever you get the time, and do songs. I did a couple of recordings, but they didn't release, they used to play in dance hall, like on dubs, and I would go and listen and go home, go out to another dance hall next night, listen again, because you're so anxious to hear your voice, you know? And keep going in the studio and going in the studio until I get "Train Is Coming," that's the first hit song that I got, right?

And in those days it was not a lotta money, it was like you workin' for a salary, you know. Sir Coxsone used to give us weekly money, you know, and if you need money to get clothes or anything like that, he gave us, Christmas comin', you know, he gave us excessive amount a money. And then, from "Train" me start to have a series of hit songs, and then Ken Boothe big. "Puppet on a String" was the first song that actually took me abroad, to England, 1967, 'cause that was the first song that actually go in foreign country and make a impact, you know? So I went to England, came back, and start, "Train," series of songs a start.

In those days, because you young and things look so nice and sound so nice, all the pleasure was in it, it wasn't like money so much, oh you love to do it, so we didn't realize that we wasn't gettin' enough for what we were doin'. And at the same time, probably him, Sir Coxsone,

KEN BOOTHE IN CONCERT
Kingston

didn't even know the business that much either, 'cause he was new into it also. He is the one who started the broad basis of it, the reggae business, music business, he is the one that really spread it wide. So at that time, he was just startin', and he probably didn't know much about the international world, etcetera, so I wouldn't say he was robbin' us any great quantity or cheatin' us any great quantity of money or anything, but I still think that we did work more than what we were gettin'. But we weren't watchin' that, we love what we were doin'. Wailers, Gaylads, Delroy Wilson, Bob Andy, Marcia Griffiths, the whole of us, was people that love what we're doin'.

At one time the whole of us fall out, we leave Sir Coxsone, 'cause all of us big enough, Delroy, Wailers, all of us is hitmakers, you know, and so the whole of us . . . in those days, singers was more together, whenever we have a problem, all of us get together like the workers in a factory, and we discuss it and we strike. We said, we don't want that, we're not gonna do that, you know? And so at one time when we and Sir Coxsone, we just couldn't get along where royalty is concerned, or rights, and so we left. We went to Beverly's, that's Leslie Kong, because Leslie Kong was the first recording outlet that start makin' international impact with the musicians in Jamaica, Desmond Dekker, Jimmy Cliff. We guys ambitious, and we decided the best place to go was Beverly's, because they are international. So all of us leave and went to Beverly's, and we did get a little better treatment.

Then again, each a these period a time, when artists realize that they still worth more, and at Beverly's we're still realizin' that they're still not givin' us enough, so we heard about Miss Pottinger, Tip Top, and we heard that she is doin' a little better, so we leave again. Royalty rights, at one point we're gettin' six cents, like fifty dollars for every thousand records, right? Then we strike again for royalties, and decided that if we don't get ten cents, we gonna stop recordin' fi alla them. And then, B. B. Seaton and myself, a lot of things that happen in Jamaica for the music, me and that guy did it, and we get no recognition for it. Nobody tell you about it. At one time me and B. B. Seaton, we would never sing a song for a man unless we gettin' ten cents. We decide that the only way that a family can survive, unless we get what we are entitled to. We keep goin', keep goin', I can't tell you all the people that we sing for, we keep breakin' the barriers, makin' thing get better and better. At one time we start getting like fifteen cents, twenty cents for a 45, and for a album we probably get fifty or so. We would check it out, we would see that the producer was gettin' it all, and then now it goes right up until I meet Lloyd Charmers. Most of these people who did recordin' those days, they didn't know nothin' about producin', their name is only on the record as producer. In those days I guess them probably didn't realize that executive producer was different from the musical producer, so they say they are producers. All right. During that period now, going up into the Seventies, there are people like Lloyd Charmers, who are musical producers who can sing, play, and know to arrange. So we heard about Lloydie again now, another steppin' stone in the business, liftin' up the music musically, not just financially. And so we all just went to him, we go into his hands, and we start to produce songs now, different kinda songs that people lookin' at in the world now, world sound, you know? Then Lloydie start workin' with Federal, that named Tuff Gong now, and out of that we get . . . my biggest hit song comes out of that, "Everything I Own," and we get "Everything I Own" number one in Europe, we got "Ain't No Sunshine," we got quite a few hit songs.

At the moment, recordin'-wise, just did an album for Jammy's. I did a album or so for New Name, this is a album that we did back over a lot of my old songs in a modern form. And the Jammy's one is all original, now, dancehall riddims, same repertoire that I used to, I don't change that, dancehall sound. 'Cause I think that the musicians in Jamaica are quite better now. Jamaican riddims. It's just the singers doin' a lotta crap, and some of the DJs, too.

Right now in the business I see it, people don't have no love anymore, people don't realize that them must help people, not fightin' people—write these thing down. Even in the music business there is corruption. Some of the people don't want to see other artists get along so that this family can survive from what we are given to do. And there are still the few that pray for each other, so we can achieve, you know? And there is the many that don't want to see no one reach anywhere. To me, got some people prayin' for you not to achieve certain thing in the business until they're ready, probably they're gonna want to give you something when you're old. Like awards and all that—I don't care about those things. I sing for God, I don't sing for money, I sing for God Almighty. I entertain man, people, but I actually sing for God, 'cause him the one that inspired me, give me this.

Right now I'm deal with my fellow man, whether you're white, you're black, you're blue, you're brown, it don't matter to me. As long as you're good, you shine the light of goodness, then you can get along. Me can't take Babylon, individual is Babylon, you know, Babylon is wickedness. And whether you're black or you're

KEN BOOTHE AT HOME
"Show me no wickedness. Cut out envy . . ."
New Kingston, May 1992

white or you're brown, if you wicked, is what me can't take, show me no wickedness. Cut out envy, 'cause that why people don't want to see other people have anything, 'cause they envious.

And some people because of the way they get brought up, and they get hurt along the way, they feel like they should hurt someone else. That's the way they get their satisfaction back. But I don't see why you should hurt a person if somebody hurts you. I think you should teach the other person about that hurt, and show them that it doesn't make sense when you hurt. God say you should do unto others as you like them to do unto you. When God say that, it's not nothin' bad him a talk about, is good things! What you love good for yourself, you must give it to other people. You should set example, so peace can come. If every man say the same thing on earth, you get peace, you know. Why it's so hard to do? Why?

Why can't them just sit down to a conference table and come to a conclusion? Why so hard for the world to live in unity and love? Some of them people sufferin' in Guatemala or them place, Ethiopia, South Africa, all over the world a people a suffer, Jamaica, and there is enough in the world that can suffice every man.

Just write these things. I never envy nobody yet in my life, never, there's nothing I want you can have materially that can strike my head that I have to envy them, or wish that they didn't have it. I'm not like that. That's why I love my parents, both my father and my mother. My father, before he died, it doesn't matter, you could have twenty cars, my father walk from his work to his house. He doesn't want to take a bus. You know what I mean? My mother just died, you know, on [May] third [1992]. You must write it, because she's a star, you know. You must write these things down. People like in my age bracket, 'cause I'm in my forties, right, our parents came from country, in the parishes. These are the real McCoy, these people. These people that came from country, like my mother, they were decent people, they were Christians. Most people that came from a parish those days, these people are real good people. All the mothers and fathers, they are the one that dyin' now, that generation that gettin' old now, that are in their nineties, their eighties, seventies. These are real McCoy, these are good people, they set an example 'cause they teach us about God, is the first thing.

Ken Boothe, Mr. Rocksteady, has been performing throughout the world for nearly three decades. His shows still drive his audiences wild with hits like "Train Is Coming" and "Everything I Own," to name a few. Constantly working, he is currently in the studio recording a new collection of hits.

LARRY MARSHALL, ORIGINAL ROCK-STEADY SINGER AND WRITER OF "NANNY GOAT"
Food, Clothes and Shelter Studio, Kingston

Winston Rodney (Burning Spear)

Since ten or fifteen years ago the music been through a lot of different phases, and there is a lot of different kind of music present itself, but then again now I think the music movin' in a proper direction. Yes, people start to reach out more for the music, people realize that they have to turn back to the original, for the original is the music that carry the substance wherein the people need to hear.

I think that when you listen to music, overall you should gain something from the music—when listening to the music, you should feel the music. It's not like you been to a concert or you buy an album and you play it today, and you can play it tomorrow, and you don't mind playing it no more. It's like you just don't wanna hear any more, y'understand. I think music should be something once you listen to it, you don't mind keep on listenin' to it because something within the music makes sense listenin' to.

Back in Europe, people like to be in touch with the original section of the music. [Music is] more rootsy, more like an art, back in Europe. Even in America, certain places, people see the music as a art, people not into this lotta DJ stuff or raggamuffin stuff or dancehall stuff. Many places in America, many of those a music reaches to a lot people, thousands of people who pay no attention to those kinda music. Places like in California, they're not into this little raggamuffin stuff and t'ing like that, more into the roots style, the heart style, y'know.

I think [my music] change [over the years] in many different ways. I think I start to get deeper and I think I start to exercise my matureness within the music. My ability within the music, my know-how within the music. I start to get deeper with the melody, some tight arangement like that. But the roots, the culture, and message is still there. With "Appointment with His Majesty" I do this song, "Loving You." I always do a little one love song here and there, it's not the kind of love people expect, but I think it's more an intelligent level of singing some love songs. The lyrics wouldn't be outrageous, 'specially elder people wouldn't mind give an ear to it; at least they hear something that they like within that form. So I think my change is for the better.

I like being on the road and being in the studio. I think both combine together. Once you present the record, and sometime peo-

BURNING SPEAR
"People have strayed from the roots, from the original understanding . . ."
New York

ple are required to want to see you. A lot of people buy our record but not see the individual, so touring is like making the connection with the people, so therefore they start to see who they have been listening to over the past years. I think touring is very important, but for me in the business since that time, I think I am looking forward to retirement. I wouldn't say in the next two or three years, but I'm lookin' within that direction. When I say "retire," I don't mean retired, period, from the music. But you wouldn't see Spear on the road touring. So that time I will spend in the studio, still creating albums, still producing my albums, and still presenting the music to the people, so people will always have music and Spear to listen to.

You haffe remember the people, for the people was there for you, y'know. And you haffe remember where you are coming from. When I like just start playing clubs with all 75 people, eighty people, in those days that was like sold out, so you have to remember your first step in the business, the way you step until you was able to make the big step, you have to remember the small step. Today many lot of young people in the music business thinkin' that they shouldn't play a club. I play at clubs. I play for people who thinkin' I wouldn't be playin' for them no more.

A club is what the whole thing was about, and every big star today can tell you what they have been through, and we all have to go through clubs before we can play a big venue or festival. Today many musician or singer may think that they can't play a place that hold only 120 people or 200 people, we cannot play for 300 people. Maybe some of these singers just have a little one song, when people may only pay attention for a couple months, then he or she may think they are so big, bigger than the song, so they are required to play in places that hold five thousand, six thousand, but when tickets start to sell and the people start to show, you can start to count: one, two, three, four, five, nobody's there. So when you coming as a young person is best to play a small place that have it packed as you can so it create a bigger vibes for you. This is how it really start. All of us have to come through some small places before we do medium places, large places, and extra large places. When you work in clubs, you feel the vibrations and that gravity from the people, and they feel it from you since they are so close, and many people would rather see you at a club more than a festival.

[When I write a song] the melody is the first thing, the melody is what write into the lyrics. So the first step is to get as much melody as you can. Sometime in your storage, when you start to store melodies, there is a lot of thing you gonna throw back through the door for you don't need those stuff, so you pick out, y'know, and break it down. So after you have all these things down, you have another time to start thinking about lyrics to fit up with the melody. It can take place any time on the road, relaxin', something just come to you, you can be eating, something come to you, anytime, it's varied. All you have to do as a musician or a singer make sure you have enough space for when it come you can accommodate it.

I would just like the people to keep in touch with Spear. As I did say before, I don't think I will always be on the road, but I think as long as Jah wish I will be in the studio. So people just keep in touch and make sure every album come out they can really reach to it and give an ear to it, for it gonna be something that makes sense listening to.

Winston Rodney, the "Man from the Hills" of St. Ann Parish, released his 29th album, Appointment with His Majesty, *in the summer of 1997. He was interviewed at his home in New York.*

CHALICE SESSION
Greenwich farm

Music Industry Version

Reggae is widely regarded as a producer's medium, and for good reason. Few reggae artists, even the most successful, are accustomed to the kind of creative control that is almost taken for granted in other genres like rock and R&B. Since the earliest days of reggae— when producers like Coxsone Dodd, Duke Reid, and Byron Lee literally controlled the market by being the only ones in Kingston with recording and pressing equipment—the producer has controlled the *sound* of reggae by creating and owning the basic tracks. He books the studio time and chooses among the never-ending stream of singers and DJs who come to his door with versions. In the hierarchy of reggae the producer is at the top; his name gets equal or greater billing than the artist. His creation, the riddim, assumes a life of its own and outlasts dozens, or even hundreds, of singer and DJ versions.

Other forms of "world music" have come and gone in the past forty years, but none have had the staying power of reggae. There are a lot of reasons, some having to do with reggae's Afro-Caribbean rhythms, lyrical content, or spiritual qualities. One major reason might be the strong music infrastructure that has been built up in Kingston by generation after generation of producers and musicians and musician-producers. While other attempts at industrial development in the Caribbean have had mixed results, reggae music has become to Kingston what country music is to Nashville and what the

JOSEPH HILL AND FRIENDS
Backstage, Cleveland

movie industry is to Bombay and Hollywood: a major economic presence as well as a focal point for local pride. Reggae is only one of many forms of popular music in the Caribbean—soca, calypso, zouk, salsa—but reggae has something that Trinidad, Martinique, Grenada, and Puerto Rico don't have. Reggae has *the factory*.

Although the effect of digital studio technology has been to strengthen the producer's hand at the expense of the musician (studio dates for drummers, in particular, remain very hard to come by), the Jamaican studio system would not function without some of the most sublime musical talent on earth. Horn players, keyboard players, guitarists, drummers, singers, self-contained bands, take your pick. When they leave on tour from Kingston's Norman Manley Airport, they carry the heart and spirit of Jamaica with them.

FREDDIE McGREGOR AND FRIENDS
Backstage, New York

MAXINE STOWE
"Reggae is very, very connected to the earth . . ."
New York, 1994

Maxine Stowe

The DJ music has fused with the rap music in America [in the Nineties], and this is instigated by this large community that has now settled in America, and the kids growing up, people like myself who came here when they were twelve, having their families and whatever. And so you find now that it has kind of created a base market that the major companies, with their interest in the music, are very connected now to the Jamaican roots. That whole rap-reggae fusion has more to do with the community, the communities living side-by-side, giving parties, and black American kids going to these parties . . . you know, that's where that amalgam is coming from. It wasn't anything instigated outside of that.

So, the music that was being put out [before], Bob Marley, Peter Tosh, that was something coming from the music companies, whereas this fusion was coming from the community. So you found that whereas the Peter Tosh and Bob Marley could not be connected back to this community, because it was, like, A&R people liking the sound, and signing the groups, and just putting them here, and just trying to cross over pop, that was the whole name of the game. Now it's the record companies trying to be "street," coming through a whole 'nother pattern, you want to be down with the community, so therefore you sign a more straightforward link. As far as what we are doing here, is that you are able now to accept all the different styles that are happening there, because you are actually becoming part of that marketplace, so you are gonna . . . even though DJ music has opened the door to the companies' interest, we are beginning to also ferret out the other styles of reggae that are down there, which is opening the door for the more creative music to come in.

Down there [in Jamaica], that's where you have the factory. What's happening up here is what's sifted through and what's able to travel, by the producer being able to travel or whatever. But down there, if you realize the way that the music is being made, it's like every day, and these artists are coming from a community that increasingly the youth have no other alternative to make a living, so every . . . like . . . you have crops and crops and crops of them, especially with the DJ styling being so easy to manipulate. Another interesting thing, I haven't really studied it, but I have this feeling that anytime the music is about to do something, the DJs come in, like the DJ, dancehall style, came in in the first place when Studio One and them started to first record. The whole DJ sound, it was in relation to the music changing from, not just being able to get records from up here and putting them on the sound systems, but actually having to make them in Jamaica, and so the DJs came in to introduce [records], whatever. And then as they started to originate and move from the ska to other styles, then the DJ started to chat more. So one interesting thing that was passing through my head when all this DJ activity started was that, actually, it was almost like . . . anytime the music needs to go somewhere, or needs to revamp itself, the DJs become prominent. And it's like, it energizes [reggae].

I was always very interested in the [singing] trios, because that was where so many of them . . . but then again, we pattern America a lot, and what was happening with the first of the music that we were listening to in Jamaica, it was all groups . . . a great percentage of it was groups. So the "group" sound, we found a lot of significance, musically we sang in groups, whether it was choirs or whatever, and then when it became . . . I guess the DJ thing brought out the more individualistic, and the hustling business also promoted the individual, because when it was more the music and the creativity, you didn't think about the business as much as you thought about the music, so you wanted to hear this fullness of sound, people would gather together in yards, and, that's how the music was made. You couldn't rush to a studio, because the studio wasn't there, so you had to do more of that, just hanging on a corner or whatever. Now you don't have to, you just hang out at Penthouse gate and try to get in. But one of the things that I wanted to do, a couple of projects that are going on down the line, are groups. And the group sound is coming back in America, too, you know what I mean?

Reggae is actually a groove, and it almost defies . . . that's how, when anybody says, dancehall music, I say this is a groove, it's a groove that you almost can take up any culture anywhere and wrap it around and spit it out, and it's the first music that has left America, went out, and came back in. Usually, you have pop music cultures in every country, but they never come back here and become successful, or go into England and become successful. But somehow, something happens with this Jamaican mix, it's able to really come back into mainstream music abroad, that other cultures have not been able to do. Like Japanese pop outside Japan, French pop, German pop, whatever, they do not sell here, but you will get a reggae pop to do well.

I would say in another three years that an international company like Sony will be able to make sense of this sound, which is a

DOMINO GAME
Nine Miles, St. Ann

JAMAICAN COUNTRYSIDE
Snake Hill, St. Catherine

groove, which as they know catches energy out of Jamaica, but can go anywhere, and also create stars in other countries, and as I say, Sony France will have a French reggae star, and Sony Italy will have an Italian reggae group, Sony Israel . . . South Africa, Lucky Dube, whatever . . . but it would be interesting if you had a major company who parlayed all that into one home, you know.

The significance of it . . . like sometimes, people say that it can be diluted, but it's not . . . when you go to Jamaica, it's going to be very hard for you to dilute it, because the people are so . . . you know, it's almost like they're rolling off the earth, you know what I mean? It's like they come up out of the dirt and they're up there, like if you go to the country you see people who seem to be coming out of the hills and coming up, so you're wondering how the hell you can ever dilute this . . . 'cause that's what's really creating the whole thing.

That's why I said that if you had a record company in Jamaica that . . . because that's what the record company does, it picks up the different shadings of things and develops it to see if it will come into something that will attract a wide audience . . . and even if it doesn't attract a wide audience, if it has a steady base . . . they will, you know, continually develop that, because they see that, if you have a steady base and you are continually developing something, something generally pops out. As long as it is credible, especially now, because people are looking for something credible . . . if you have some credibility going on, you stand a chance in this environment. People, I guess, are looking more than just retro in their thinking.

I am interested to see what the impact of the music is gonna be on the Jamaican audience, because that's where everything is going to bubble out of. If the environment in Jamaica gets more structured, like you have songs, you have promotion . . . the consumer, how that affects his diet, his acceptance of music and so forth . . . that will feed into what actually comes out of the studios as popular music. 'Cause whatever is popular music out of Jamaica is what's going to be selling to all these communities. So, you're never gonna have a breakdown, like what happened before, if you stay connected to that, so wherever it changes, you just go with it. I know that there's a clamoring now in the society for a more melodic, creative . . . like, there's a sincere longing. People are getting tired of the same rehashed stuff.

I think the whole [reggae] thing is like a spiritual experience, myself, because I've always been motivated by community concerns, worried about the health of the community. With that kind of con-

SUGAR CANE FIELD
Snake Hill, St. Catherine

sciousness, it makes it easier for reggae to come in, because people's minds are prepared to know how to deal with that music, because the harshness of everyday life, and the driving monotony, it's getting to them . . . because they feel that they are technically destroying the world, that they actually are looking for some kind of space where they can regenerate themselves, and the reggae music is just like the beaches of Jamaica, you can just go out there and . . . like . . . the demons [go away].

It's the same for any music, it's just that, for me, the Jamaican music, you're dealing with people who are just rolling off the land, who have not been disconnected from it, like . . . I feel that I am disconnected, so I have to go after the specific things to get connected, whereas they just live connected. So their interpretations or their art forms, my embrace of them kind of keeps me connected to that.

You know, Jamaica's really an agricultural [country] . . . most of the population lives very close to the land. If you take one of those small planes from Kingston to MoBay, you can't believe where people have houses . . . you see a house on a mountaintop, and a little track, people existing there, cut off from the rest of the world. They form the spirit of the country. That's why . . . you go to other places in the Caribbean, and it's nice, the beach is nice, the people are nice, but everybody who comes to Jamaica, there is another thing going there, like another energy coming out of that place, that's . . . it's quirky, you keep feeling more refreshed, you just get a more a sense like you've been somewhere. They're very, very connected to the earth.

As I tell them [at Sony], you have to have a studio in Jamaica. You have to have your hand in there. Because so many of the studios down there are owned by the producers, and you have to depend, you have to get studio time, it can get very tricky. If this company opens a studio in Jamaica, it will create more fusions happening down there. Another interesting thing is that, if the industry really develops in Jamaica, structurally, you will find that other music styles out of the Caribbean will begin to feed through more readily, because Jamaica will become a spot where you can go for you to go further.

Maxine Stowe, an executive with Island Jamaica and formerly affiliated with Sony Music, got her start working with her uncle, Studio One owner Clement "Coxsone" Dodd. She was interviewed in New York.

Chalice

WAYNE ARMOND: Unfortunately, the reggae bands out of Jamaica, who are self-contained reggae bands, they're just four of us, and two of us are over ten years old—Third World going on eighteen years, Chalice is in its eleventh year, Bloodfire is about eight years now, and then Mystic Revealers, who happen to be the newest. The rest are back-up groups, you know, or singers. I think one of the problems with it is the economics of the situation. Youngsters today would want to form a group, right, but first of all equipment is a heavy load financially, second of all to be a self-contained group, you're not gonna get that many breaks. You can put a band together now, any musician can put a band together and back artists. They can go on tour with Shabba, they can back Culture, they can go with Burning Spear, all those artists who don't have a regular band. For a youngster looking for opportunity to travel and seeking to make a quick buck, it's better to form a backing group.

It's hard to say what direction reggae going in. What it's en-compassin' is very old Jamaican music—*mento, poco,* you know, all the ethnic music from early Jamaica, only this is now being played on a drum machine, but the influences are valued. You do research and you go back into the archives and listen to some of those old-time ethnic sounds from Jamaica. You hear them in dancehall music. Not the old Studio One beats, further back than that. Before reggae, before even the advent of ska or rock steady. I'm talking about the things they call *burru,* way, way back from my great-grandfather in slavery days, that's what we're talking about. And those rhythms, we call them cultural now, if you go to a festival show and you see the people in the Jamaican band and a thing, you hear the same thing, the same feel as the dancehall rhythms.

I was just by accident involved in Carnival this year. I happened to know Denyse Plummer, who is a popular Trinidadian calypsonian, and she was on Byron Lee's truck—I used to work with Byron Lee for awhile—so Byron Lee invited me on the truck, right. So I was there on the truck and started to play with soca music, and when I saw the sea of people all around, what amazed me was there were no acts of violence. There were people jammed together for miles. They were happy people, they were not cussin', there was no bottle-throwin', there was no gun firin'. And when we reach down in Half Way Tree, they start to play a soul calypso beat, and I change

CHALICE AT HOME, NEW KINGSTON
(*left to right*) Wayne Armond, Mikey Wallace, Keith Francis,
Wayne "C-Sharp" Clarke, Alla, Dean Stephens.

the riddim, I start to play this new "Bam Bam" riddim on the soul calypso beat, and the singers on the truck started to sing everything from Tiger to Papa San to it, and we change it into reggae, and it worked so beautiful, great combination.

Two things it make me think of—the music is so universal, there is no dividin' line between reggae and soul calypso, it's just Caribbean music, and people love both forms; second thing that it make me think about was why these people come out to soca, come on the street, jump up with one another, dance around, feel good about music, no acts of violence, no bottle-throwin', and these are the same people who goin' into the dance hall, and they wild with violence in the dance hall. It make me wonder what go on in the dance hall—this gun violence, this kind of anarchy thing that happenin' in the dance hall, you know, the killer soundboy, the gun 'pon you, the dibi this one and dis that one. As far as that is concerned, in the reggae music, I'd like to see that stop. I think that the DJs can make it stop. And a testament to this is Tiger and Papa San, two DJs who never talk 'bout gun this and gun that, and have been out the longest apart from Yellowman, have been around for five years. For a DJ that's a long life.

ALLA: I think of music in two ways. I think of music the art and I think of music the business. Now, part of the problem with the reggae is that there was not enough business. Now for the next ten years, some of us have realized that this business is most necessary, so we're working on things like that, so there are gonna be changes in that arena. Where the music is concerned now, as the art, like everything else, if it stands still, it means it's going back. So there has got to be change for you to have growth. To me, this is what the reggae needs to do—to spread itself out. Reggae should not only be this and if it's not this, it's not reggae. It should be reggae growing, stretching out its tentacles, branching out like a tree.

[Recycling of old riddims] for me is one of the major problems with the music of today. OK, copying something is the best form of flattery, which is fine. But what happens? You have to realize that these people left a legacy, so you could take this and use. Now, what is happening is they are not leaving any legacy for the next genera-tion. That to me is a very serious problem, is something that has to be addressed. And without a doubt there are people out there that feel the same way I do, are willing to do something about it. You have to grow, which is what music has been about all along. Art has always been like that, art has always been influences. And because of its influences, then it influence other things.

CHALICE REHEARSING
"We are into a different cycle now, and it's going to change . . ."
Kingston, April 1992

Influences cause you to influence other people. If you do something reggae with a little Brazilian, then it's easier for the Brazilian people to accept this, because it touches them instantly: "There is something I can relate to." Although it has a different color inside of it. You're used to red, so put a little blue in it, but there's still the red that I am used to, so I know the red, but this blue gives it a slightly different hue, and I like this. It is a path that we have to take now for our necessary growth, because without growth then all it do is die. There's no standing still, 'cause once you stand still you are regressing.

I don't worry so much. For me, I find that there are cycles. Life has cycles. We are into a different cycle now, and it's going to change. You will find you get an influx of musicians again. You have all the technology, and, very soon, people will say, "Oh, well, this is all it is, let's go somewhere else." And this is what comes. When you consider what's been happening for the past five or six years, to hear that drum now live is fresh. Sometimes I go into the studio now, and I find that the engineers there have gotten so used to the drum machines that they don't even know how to mike a drum properly. So you go in and say, "mike this drum," it's something they are learnin'. It will return. Singers cannot be replaced. Even musicians cannot be replaced by all of this technology, because somebody has got to program it. The ideas have got to come from somewhere.

I'm a hopeful person. I have hope that things will change. The world has been through lots of different cycles, and it keeps going around. Important things always rise eventually. There have been times when it has been subjugated, and then it rise again. The age of the Renaissance, and so on, it just prove. There's darkness, then light comes in, then you get a little darkness again. Maybe is just for us, so we can appreciate the light.

MIKEY WALLACE: Ever since the beginning of reggae music, it has been to get people movin' and jammin' and listenin'. You go to other countries, people don't understand the words, but they're jammin' on it and dancin' on it, sometimes even singin' along, even if they can only catch one word. I've been listening to Brazilian music, African music, and as long as there's a groove to it, I'm enjoyin' it. There's magic in it, and I guess I just want to keep the magic in the music.

Chalice's original songs and dynamic stage show have won them fans everywhere.

DENNIS BROWN, THE REIGNING "KING" OF REGGAE SINGERS
New York, May 1992

Carlene Davis

To me reggae is definitely moving forward. We cannot deny what has taken place in the past with the likes of Bob Marley, Peter Tosh, and all those, but we have to realize that it's a whole new generation, you know, that is now in the forefront or is moving towards the forefront, and they have new ideas, new feeling. It's just like in the Sixties, when the hippie was happening, they were thinking on a level, Vietnam War was on, and they were all concerned about peace. I think this generation now, they're a little mixed up, they're not sure which way to go, so it is all coming out in the music. Some are very much into street living, the drugs, the guns; others are still very steadfast on dealing with peace, and the whole thing of staying away from drugs, trying to live a straight life, so you're getting all that mixed up in the music, lyrically, and rhythmically. I think it keeps getting better, because the beat is tightening up, so that just about everyone can dance to it.

[Female reggae artists] are still climbing. There are a lot of singers out there, and in the last two years, a lot of young energetic singers have come forward. At one time, if I might say so, I felt I was the only one that was doing the kind of music I was doing, 'cause everybody was very much into the roots stuff, and I was dabbling in just about anything that was great music. But I'm glad to see there are a lot more singers coming forward, and producers are looking at them. They're enthused about working with female artists where before it was a big no-no. Not only that, the younger girls are more positive about themselves, and I think that is through dancehall music, you know, whatever is happening in dancehall has really encouraged a lot of the young singers to come forward.

A lot of stuff that is done for Jamaica wouldn't do well abroad, and then you'll find the odd one that will just do great things abroad, it's big here and America picks it up, or Europe. It comes down to promotion, great promotion. I think that's what has held back a lot of great artists and great music, not having the right source behind you to get you into the right places. I know my music is in all those territories that you mention [Europe, Japan]; it's just that, like I said before, without proper promotion you reach them on a lukewarm level instead of full force. You go and you make an impact and you realize that people like you; now you don't want to go back without having the support behind you the next time. You want to

CARLENE DAVIS
Couch Studios, Kingston

go back strong, so that they can't refuse you. So that's why I've held off doing a lot of tours.

I think Europe was always there for good music, I still believe that Europe is the kind of place that . . . they can read through you. Europeans are a very intimate crowd, they can feel you out and know whether you're really for real, not that you are a one-shot. They will give a brand-new artist an opportunity to go out there, but you have to deliver your stuff. But if you're true to what you're doing and show the potential and the honesty in the music, they'll be there for you all the time.

Reggae can only go up from here, and it has to be straight up, and I'll try to make sure it does that.

Carlene Davis is one of Jamaica's top recording and performing artists.

809 BAND
(*front, left to right*) Dean Fraser, Desi Young, Chico Chin
(*rear, left to right*) Bo-Pee Bowen, Nambo Robinson, Gibby Morrison, Michael Fletcher, Paul Kastick

809 Band

NAMBO ROBINSON: I think the quality is improving, and there's a looking back on the kind of stuff that was done, the older stuff, and based on that standard, people are beginning to reshape this new sound and new riddims and to make more quality sound and expression. I see a greater future. Computer will be there, but I think it will be used more creatively then. They're coming back to the horns, you know, coming back to the acoustic drum kit, and to me that is a great improvement in terms of thinking.

We see a great future for the music. It's becoming more popular in places, like even Guam, other islands in the Pacific, India, Japan. The music, it is growing, steadily. We want to assure people that the music is alive and well.

DEAN FRASER: The music escalate all the time. It have never stopped. Regardless of what people want to think, or might think, I think that the music that really happenin', that music is out there doin' its work. We did a tour recently with Freddie McGregor. We record recently, this one, it should be on MTV soon, because they were asking for the rights for one of the songs.

The music overall hasn't really left off in any great way; it's just that the dancehall have moved to the forefront. But the music is always there. The Mighty Diamonds make good records, so does Culture, Black Uhuru, so do we—809 Band—so the music is always there. It's just dancehall is what is in the forefront right now. People tend to forget that.

809 Band was Jamaica's hardest-working back-up band. 809 also recorded and released original material under its own name.

David Hinds (Steel Pulse)

Yellowman was probably the next thing that came after Bob Marley, and I think that was a turning point in the direction of reggae music, where it started to become dancehall, and not only that, that the lyrical content started to dwindle, it was goin' on the wane as far as I was concerned. No disrespect to Yellowman, because even to this present day, I still find him as one of the most energetic performers to come out of Jamaica. But in all honesty, like I said, it was also the beginning of an era of a lot of negativity in the music.

I often ask myself about things, how they work. For example, I'm no marijuana smoker, but, at the same time, that was the big thing that was happening around the time when [Steel Pulse] were involved with the music that everybody knows us for today. And along with that sort of thing that was happening, the music also had a certain level of consciousness, because it was taken in a context where everybody's into meditation, reasoning, and really taking a look at nature, and being thankful for the things that God has provided for some years. When the whole marijuana, Rastafari philosophy phased out, you find that harder drugs was comin' in, and a lack of consciousness as well.

So, we've been led to believe as a people that the music, or what we used to do with the music before, was influencin', like a bad influence on the young ones comin' up, because of our Rasta, long hair, drugs, against the system, and you know, the educated fools put that propaganda out there that it wasn't good for the people. Now, since then, they've succeeded in phasin' it out for a point, and they've allowed the harder drugs comin' in, and also a lot of negativity in the lyrics, and also a stagnant musical format as well, because since Marley died as well, there was a lot of music that came out there, that was a million versions of one song. 85 versions of Sleng Teng, 100 riddims of [another], now we've got about the fortieth version of one of the Bogle tracks, you know, that sort of thing, and I think, Thank God for bands like ourselves, not blowin' my own trumpet, and a few others that have tried to keep on the straight and narrow, knew what the game was, and we kept goin' and kept on goin' until we've arrived here.

So over the years, the only advance I think the dancehall had from, say, ten years ago to now is that it was a form of music that replaced reggae music as we knew it back in the early Eighties. But

DAVID HINDS—PRESIDENTIAL INAUGURATION
Washington, D.C., January 1993

DAVID HINDS
Rehearsal, N.Y.C., 1993

I'm grateful that it's replaced it to this point, only to this point, for the fact that we needed some kind of music out there to still compete with the other types of musical categories like your R&B, your pop, and your rock. Reggae needed some kind of format there, but unfortunately, like the moods that came with it was a lot of negative lyrics, and it's only probably the last couple of years now we found that there are a few artists who are trying to say positive things back on the music again. I'm wondering how much damage has been done now, that it can't be repaired.

Another advantage came out of [dancehall] is that, for once, that the voice of the people in the ghetto is being heard on another level now. The people are relying on the DJs with the messages now, they're relying on the DJs and the dancehall musicians now to educate them and tell them what's happening, as opposed to reading the papers and listening to the bull that the politicians are coming up with now. I don't mind the DJs talk about guns, because I've been back to Jamaica; I don't think there was one day I picked up the newspaper without seeing somebody shot, so that's real. What I'm really against is talking about something that's degradin' women, and there's no solution to. Something that's . . . constantly keep the woman down, without any solution . . . I find it gets to be tedious after a while, especially when there's a lot more important issues on the island, and more important issues generally.

The music has reached a stage where you have British reggae, and you have reggae from Jamaican artists that came to America and write their songs and record their songs, and you have the reggae that's from Jamaica. Now, the way the music is growing now, the reggae that's going on in Jamaica, or dancehall reggae, I think they've got it all sewn up now, in a bag, where even ourselves have to be lookin' towards Jamaica for the direction—not that we never did before, but now more than ever before, you know. I've been 'round to a few studios, and the sound is so tight there, I can't really imagine recording anywhere else, and turn around and try to compete against a Jamaican track now, because I think they've got it all tied up now. The sound is so tight, they know exactly what kind of sounds to give each musician, and whether you like the songs or not, you find yourself just rockin' to the grooves, because they've got the grooves in the pocket now. Sly Dunbar is one of the forerunners of that.

You find out that the record companies, now, you see they appreciate the sounds that are coming from Jamaica and a lot of them are gonna begin to set bases up down there, coming down with all of their office help so they can scout 'round for new artists. And that's why there has been this new wave of signing a lot of acts, like the Buju Bantons and the Cobras and the Ninjamans and the Shabba Ranks, because they've been down there now, and they've seen that . . . you know, they're not just getting better musically, but they're getting a lot more organized as well.

That's another thing that I noticed down there, is they are more business-orientated, the producers are getting a lot more clout, and some of them are going to publishing deals with major acts, which . . . I think it's going to be around for a long time, now. We have to root out certain negative things, like the coke scene that's grown up, that's done a lot of damage as well; a lot of very great acts have fallen to that, unfortunately.

Up until probably the past five years, before five years ago, let's say, Japan had a very strong respect for the Western world influences, musically, and, if [record companies] said, "Look, it's fried ice cream with roasted onions, which is the flavor of the month," the Japanese would just shake their heads and say, "Yeah, you're right," and go ahead and order a million copies of fried ice cream and roasted onions. And I think the Japanese have started to come to Sunsplash, for example, appreciating the music, and beginning to realize that they don't have to be having the Western world influences—who have been keeping reggae music down for a long time, as well, I might add—and they've been out there, and they're signing their acts themselves, because they see the potential.

We went to Japan earlier, in '92, and it was pretty evident that Japanese people—I mean, they've heard us for some time on record—but it was pretty evident that they didn't quite hear this kind of reggae music before. You know, 'cause all the acts that have been goin' over has been your dancehall acts, and all of a sudden they're hearing things where there's fusion, there's different styles and different coordination of music, horns, messages, and, you know, it was like a direct show conducted there. And they might have stopped for a second and said, "Wow!" I think the Japanese people were very impressed when they saw us.

David Hinds is leader of Steel Pulse (founded in Birmingham, England in the Seventies), one of the oldest and best-known British reggae groups.

LEROY "HORSEMOUTH" WALLACE
Legendary drummer and star of the 1978 film *Rockers*
Kingston, 1992

Jack Radics

I think musically, there has been a regression, personally, you know, 'cause five or ten or fifteen years ago, the artists and the musicians were creative then. Today, even though we have the advantage of the computer technology and all'a that to enhance . . . but because these things simplify so much, it has lost the creative edge, cause we still, all we doin' is recyclin' stuff that was made fifteen, twenty years ago. As it relates the business thing, I think maybe today's crop of artists have a greater awareness of the music business and the intricacies of it than the generation of artists before. The business is now more and more becoming an industry, getting more and more formalized, here in Jamaica. And that's good. All in all, we have grown.

The people that are coming into the business as producers or executive producers, for all of the artists it's an advantage, you know, 'cause here's another paymaster, so that's another payday for you. OK, yes, fine, but that's a short term, because in the long run it does a greater disservice to the overall longevity of the music, and it's lifespan—I don't know if I'm making sense here, right—but from where I stand, you know, there is so much non-musical people comin' into the business, with a lot of capital, wanting to find some way to rinse it or launder it, or set up a front to get legit, or whatever, you know, sure, fine, that means more food for all of us artists, but what does it do to the music?

That goes back to the point that I was making about the regression of the creativity . . . all right, here we are: it is unfortunate that the supposed biggest marketplace in the world, America, and I say it, "supposed," because I don't buy that for one minute, right? It is uncanny that the aspect of reggae that they choose to embrace and market and sell is just the entertainment aspect of reggae. Right? Now, the basic thing about music is that it must entertain, fine, but it must also inform and educate, right?

Now, just like in the time of Bob Marley and Burning Spear and Culture and all these people, Mighty Diamonds, it was more the Europeans, and the Africans, and the Asians that gravitated toward the music in its true form. That is the *music*, that is the creative aspect of the music. Today those people still compose songs, but the companies that are signin' and buyin' supposed talent, they're not interested in all these people. Them interested in the mass-produced shit.

JACK RADICS
"You have to keep nurturing the roots . . ."
Kingston, 1993

It's the smallest outlay for the smallest return, and I guess because we are Third World people and Third World artists, we just get treated real shitty, you know. Record companies sign you for the cheapest budget, and then even when you get 150,000 U.S. dollar, I mean, come on, rap groups use that to make a single. You know, you supposed to get an advance to make a hit album with at least four or five hit singles off it, just havin' the money to groom yourself and make yourself marketable . . . come on, it's not happenin'. So, to me, it's like it's some kind of a token gesture—it's buyin' out what could upstage you, buyin' out the competition. The commitment to the artistic development isn't there.

I remember, in all my years of trying to get hooked up with a major label, etcetera, etcetera, I'd always been told, "Oh, we don't know how to market this." I submitted them a tape with songs of a ballad nature, dark nature, hard-core reggae, lovers' rock. I submit a variety of things, and they would be, like, "What direction do you want to pursue," and I'd say, "What do you mean, what direction? I don't want to be stereotyped. I'm an artist. I'm a singer. It's about music, and you can't categorize me, and go, 'there's a ballad singer, there's a reggae singer.'" That's just the segregationist mentality, apparently, that inherited from fuckin' colonialism, or some shit, I don't know. Divide and rule. It's the same principle. You don't hear reggae on Top 40 radio; it's a specialist thing. There's no integration.

We as artists and singers and players of instruments, we have that power, it is us that command the ears and the hearts and the minds of the people, you know, not the politician or the clergymen, because they have long realized the disillusionment of alla that.

I remember, when I was a teenager in the Seventies, you know, you had training centers, you could aspire to be something, you could be a mason or a mechanic or . . . you understand? Today those centers, them cease, and so the youths in the ghetto, it's the gun or the mike that is your salvation, right? Even in today's world, it's like, you wonder what is required there. Everyday, everybody is up in arms about the music and the sex and the violence and alla this that it portrays, and still, the powers that be and that determine the marketplace, they still embrace it and that is what them want to sell. There's no encouragement for us who want to make music of a particular level, because it don't get played, it don't get marketed, you know, "Oh, we don't know how to market this."

It can only get better, because, like I said before, the current crop of artists—it's the changing of the guard, so to speak—has a different awareness level of the business, and I think even the current crop of DJs are thinkin' melodies, are thinkin' arrangements, thinkin' musical as opposed to just commercial. I think that the future will be good. I think even the record companies are . . . after that first wave of euphoria or whatever . . . when them come back to earth, I think some of them are realizing now, but some of them must still find out. The picture is being painted much clearer now, like them placing more interest in the music than in the fad. You can understand the fad still, you know. As a businessman, you can understand that level, but it should not be at the cost of the music. You can't have the leaf at the cost of the root, you know, you kill the tree. Well then, that must be your intention, and there must be ulterior motives afoot, we wonder. So you have to keep nurturing the root, you know.

I think all them companies that come sign people, they should have signed Bunny Wailer and Beres Hammond and all them people there. But those are the people them don't want to sign, that them don' wan' big-up, because that's the music that attacks the same establishment that them are bastion and pillar and stone of. It's like Catch-22, damned if you do, damned if you don't. So what do we do? We just make the music, make the music speak. The longer you suppress somethin', when it emerges, or submerges, or whatever the grammar is for that, it will have so much lava at such infinite depth, that's the power at the music.

The thing is, what we need here in Jamaica, what reggae music business need, is the people in the business need to be educated about the business, and when I say the people in the business, I'm talkin' about artist, engineer, producer, executive producer, booking agent, management, the whole level. There is nobody that spent their money and went to any college or university to take a course in this thing. It's all on-the-job training at the artists' expense, and me as an artist observe, "We tired 'a aid them," you know what I'm sayin'? Somebody have to decide to provide some kind of public awareness. I don't know what, but every time I go in a meeting with the hierarchy, I always try and say, "Let's have a place down at the library, or a place down at the cultural arts center, or somewhere where you can learn music business, music education, and different thing." That is my aim. My aim in life would be to have some kind of institution of that nature, because I was fortunate to be a part of such an institution when I lived in England, and the knowledge and expertise and everything that I gained from that was tremendous, you know. It is what makes me who and what I am today, my whole awareness of the thing. It is unfortunate that within the business, as a whole, politics have its advantage, because the more you know, the less you can be manipulated, and the less you can be manipulated, the less you are lied to, you know.

What we need is more information, we need to start an information service industry for the business. I don't know if somebody, after reading this, will want to take the challenge, you know, because it's something I've been trying to get government involvement with for years, and everybody says, "Oh, yes, put it on paper, send us a proposal," but nobody really works unless it's a private entity.

Look at the copyright law. This is a law we've had since 1911, the whole provision was from 1911, I mean, we were British subjects. And our first independent government have in its cabinet a man who was the promoter and producer of Jamaica's first international hits, and him never see fit to secure copyright legislation. And several governments have changed and that said individual has even become prime minister! And still, to no avail. It may be poetic justice that we have change in prime minister now, he has really brought it to bear. Wonderful, praise the Lord. If they were interested, it shouldn't take thirty-odd year. When them want to change a bill for tax them change it in *lane*, you know what I'm sayin'? It leaves you wonderin'.

However, that's water under the bridge. We are here now and it's here, and we'll see how it works, because we need it. We need the protection for our creativity, that is the pension, because we have certain rights. Even though we pay taxes, we're not getting a pension from the government. It is our publishing and those rights which are our pension. It's artistry, that's your art. All in all, we're looking good in the 2000s, and hope we can do some benefit.

Singer Jack Radics was interviewed at his home in Kingston.

GREGORY ISAACS
New York, 1992

Bobby "Digital" Dixon

Reggae in the Nineties, explosion! Breakin' barriers, winnin' people together, worldwide. No matter where in the world you are, there is a place for reggae. Anywhere on the globe, anywhere you turn, there is a little spot, and that spot is gradually expandin'. A big expansion program is goin' on. You are surprised, in Spanish, Greek, French, it's there. If the language really doesn't catch on, that pulsatin' beat that it got, it really make you have to move.

Reggae got a lot of potential, but what it really need is some good promotion, some backing from the companies abroad, who know that a company can really finance and promote the artists. That is what the business really need internationally, you know. Promotion. In the States now, reggae don't play for more than a segment of a program. It not part of their daily routine. You find radio stations playing reggae intermix in their slots, not like you find them play six reggae songs in straight or so, but they'll have a little slot where they'll put in one or two songs. That is the way it is played now, but that is really good still for the business, because it is gettin' international exposure, and a more wider variety of people hear it when it is played on those stations. In the earlier day, that would never happen.

In Jamaica, even five years ago, you didn't hear reggae on the radio, like you were in the States. Now, we have Irie-FM—that was a great achievement, that help promote a lot of kids that you never thought of and heard of, and even if their song don't sell number one, yet it get a chance to be proven by the public. If the public say, "Yes, I heard that song on Irie, gonna get it," well, at least it get a chance. Before, a man produce a song, you walk 500 mile or so tryin' to get one sell or tryin' to get it promoted or something, and it just wasn't in the favor of the artist and the producer, 'cause producer spend a whole lot of money and the song don't go anywhere.

The technology really explain a great part of putting out better productions and stuff, you know. Technology have increased worldwide, so you find that with the technology increasin', then you will know that the reggae music itself is increasing. Well, you find that it is going places. Reggae is right out there takin' over the United States, apart from the R&B, and you know that reggae is catchin' on all over the world, so you find that the style have to be creative.

BOBBY DIGITAL
"Reggae in the Nineties, explosion! . . ."
Digital B Studio, Kingston

That's why you find all different sort of sounds and beats, you know, it is creativity.

You might say every year you hear a different sound, but you got to give the people what they want. The now generation, which is lookin' out for the music and which is buyin' the music, you got to cater for the people. If, say, Bob Marley is a legend, Bob Marley did what he came here to do, so I don't think every one should be lookin' out to see another Bob Marley, right, because Bob Marley has played his part, Burning Spear, Bunny Wailer, Peter Tosh, Jimmy Cliff, on those track. There are a lot of other young artists which is comin' and goin' in that direction also, right, but you see it's just a matter of time. In the first instance when the rock music were in the States, people were saying, "Cho, that's nothin', that's a waste," and now it has dominated. So reggae have its payday, it don't matter what the artist might be.

Groups are good, a lot of good groups here, right? A lot of good groups. Name all the groups, reggae groups, they are still here. Culture, Burning Spear, Diamonds, Heptones, Tamlins, everything. They are still here. But they need promotion, seen? True, some of them really out of the biz for a few years, but they are here, and now, what I am seeing, they are in the studios doing fresh recordings, sound just the same, talent is there, so there is nothing to say. Well then, artist is out. Because of lack of recording, they are out of touch of the biz. Some of them may be going through difficult time in the biz, so they try to choose another career or something, but the groups like Fullness, the singers like Johnny Clarke, they are still here.

The good things, the good songs of the past will never die, you see, because the now generation, like the older folks, if they should go to a dance now and hear those [older] songs, they just automatically remember those days, so automatically, those old songs when they play in the dance and the younger folks hear them, they say, "Yes! Wicked song! Good song!" because it is a song of the past, but it lives on. So same like now, the songs of the Nineties, if there is a good song in the lot, couple years time, the younger folks in those time comin' up, they will really accept that song also, like how we accept a Bob Marley song, a Heptones song. We just know that a good song is a good song, and you really have to give it credit.

Bobby "Digital" Dixon was coproducer of Shabba Ranks's Grammy Award–winning album, As Raw As Ever. *Currently, he is working with Sizzla and Morgan's Heritage. He was interviewed at his studio in Kingston.*

THE MIGHTY DIAMONDS (BUNNY, TABBY, JUDGE)
S.O.B.'s, New York City, 1994

Don Taylor

I used to tell artists that when you make a record, you're in direct competition with—if you're going international—with Prince, Michael Jackson, 'cause you're fightin' for that airplay, so you've got to . . . you cannot make a third-quality record and go up against Michael Jackson for airplay; you're not gonna get played. So I think they're understanding that. And I think that, if one or two more dancehall artists can emerge with quality records, and do same direction that Shabba Ranks has, I think that they could get a ten-year run out of this dancehall and it could progress into other things. And one of the main reasons for dancehall being popular, which just came to my attention, is that most of your rap kids in New York, whether it's Chuckie D with Public Enemy, or KRS-1, or Heavy D, all of a sudden, everybody thought all these guys were Americans, but as soon as they became rich, they said, "No, I'm from Jamaica, I'm from Antigua, my mother's from so-and-so, I like to eat ackee and codfish," you know what I mean? All of a sudden they are identifying themselves, and they want to identify with the music, so it gives the music an additional life.

Like, you can't find a record in New York now, a rap record, where the people don't say "Shabba Rankin'," "Me and my man Shabba Rankin'." He's gettin' advertising, publicity, he couldn't pay for. Yes! And people are coming to his shows. I did a show with him in L.A., and Heavy D came over, Ice Cube came over, and performed with him for free. He's now the hip thing and they want to be part of what's hip.

Because there is a new exodus in travel, it's easier for [Jamaican] ghetto kids, legally or illegally, to get to the United States and get exposed to both the good and the bad of the United States. They have become more aware of what the music business is about. They still don't quite have it, but at least now, you can't come to them and give them $10,000 or $20,000 for an album and publishing and stuff. He still may not know what publishing is, but he knows it's two separate deals, OK? Which was not around then. And they also have learned something they didn't know about, which is called quality control. The mere fact that they have managers now, they have lawyers, now you talk to a Jamaican artist, they go, "Talk to my manager, talk to my lawyer." That didn't exist.

DON TAYLOR
"*When you enter the race, you've got to know what the prize is . . .*"
Kingston, 1994

Black music in America, when I started, it was called "race" music, then it was R&B, we had a little chart for that. But you know what kept us going? It's that the artists were much better performers than the mainstream artists. It's a long ride, but you kept building. Nobody thought Michael Jackson was gonna be as big . . . the record company didn't think he was gonna be that big . . . only Michael did. He said, "The only tool I have, is every time they give me a shot on TV, I'm gonna be better than the last time. I'm gonna be better than the last time." Because that's the only shot that you're gonna get—record companies is not gonna spend the money marketing an African American, or an African-descended artist, like they would do in the early stages of a white artist. The African-descended artist first have to prove that he can sell records, then they'll take some of the profit and invest it back. But they're not gonna spend a million dollars on a campaign like they do for a white act.

We are taught that we have no segregation in America, but the music business is definitely segregated. You go into a record company, and this is the black department, this is the white department, and they don't intermingle. The black guy got to convince this white guy why he should get his record played for him. Same thing on the other side. Most reggae acts get signed by a white department. Third World people, especially Jamaicans, they still have this thing that if the white guy sign you, [success] is automatic. So they don't understand that they've got to make a relationship with the black guy. So when the white guy sign the black guy, he says to the black guy, "What am I gonna do with this?" The artists don't have a manager that's known in the black community, so there's no rapport. What Shabba did, he went and played the rapper conventions, and he was around, and everybody got to know him. Now Shabba Ranks is not a Jamaican; he's part of the American hip-hop music scene, he's one of us, they consider him, and that makes a good difference.

You see, music biz I look at as a race. When you enter the race, you've got to know what the prize is. You can't wait to get to the finish line to ask what the prize is. That's what happened with most Jamaican artists. They enter the race, they sign the contract, and then they get to the finish line, and they say, "Now, what do I get?" By that time the race is over, and it's not what they expected to get. You've got to ask at the start of the race, "What is the prize if I get to the end of this thing?"

Don Taylor, Bob Marley's personal manager from 1973 to 1980, has handled the careers of many reggae and R&B artists in his more than thirty years in the music business.

LATE NIGHT SESSION
Anchor Recording, Kingston

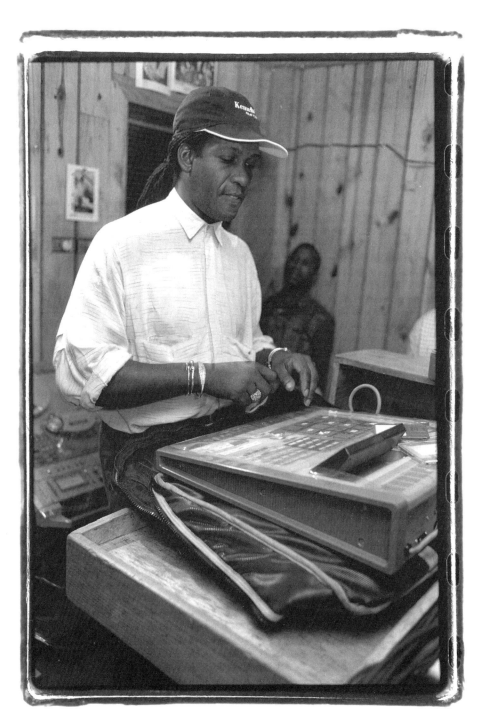

SLY DUNBAR
"Strictly some wicked grooves . . ."
Kingston, 1992

Sly Dunbar

It's the world beat thing now, it's comin' up, comin' to the forefront. People are just dancin' to riddim, and I think what happen now, all music seems similar right now at this moment. I think it just a beat sometime, a tempo sometime that differ. Everything is coming in, like Latin, African, Indian kind a music, Japanese, everything is coming together as one. So I think reggae is gonna be big, if we get the proper songs and the proper melody and stuff like that, 'cause the beat is there, and everybody loves it, just incorporate the different sounds of the world, makin' it great, and not just copyin' everything. I think that probably is a bit boring right now, we keep on cuttin' that old style like we can't make anything new, and it's a bit boring. So I think if we can create, then we can stay.

I try to do a bunch of different stuff, 'cause I'm just trying to figure what the people want to hear and what they're tired of hearin', you know. You can't always do it the same way, sometime people don't want to hear it. Even the riddim of "Bam Bam," the "Bam Bam" riddim, can't do it all the time.

People can relate to the riddim, 'cause everything start from the drums and all. Brazilian music, Caribbean music, African music, all the music I can think of, the drum is always the major source, and if the drums and percussion is rhythmic, the people can dance, then you have a winner. People just want to dance, they want anything they can just move to. And once that is in the music, I think, the singer can go on top of it and do it good. You have to incorporate it within the reggae.

I think reggae into the Nineties is gonna be African oriented, rhythmically, it's just gonna be percussive, just grooves, strictly some wicked grooves, not overplaying on top of the riddim, just playin' what the riddim needs, and not overproducing, a simple groove that a nine-years-old kid can understand. Different percussion, even if the bass drum is going straight, but the other things on top of it don't distract you from the major groove that is there, not overproducing, playing simple, playing less, but at the same time is very effective.

Recorded versions of Sly Dunbar riddims have been riding the charts in Jamaica for many years. Some of Sly's productions include the massive Beenie Man hit "Foundation" as well as the "Mission Impossible" rhythms. His most recent album is La Trenggae *on his Taxi label. He was interviewed in Kingston, April 1992.*

JAH SCREW
"Most people is not confident to do something new . . ."
Kingston, May 1992

Jah Screw

Right now in the States, is more happenin' for reggae, you know, everybody's imbibing reggae nowadays. How it's gonna go into the Nineties, reggae given the chance, like more major company, airplay, it's gonna happen for reggae, it's definitely gonna happen, 'cause you see it's happening with Shabba already. It happen before, for people like Yellowman, him get a good response where the world is concerned. So it's gonna happen. At the moment, you have a big market for the roots, you have a big roots market, but it's way out there. You're not hearing Burnin' Spear up upon the forefront at the moment, but he's there. When he perform in Paris or New York, the crowds come, it's a packed house.

Some of the thing that we are doing is, a little bit of African styles in the drummin', we're mixin' it, puttin' in all the flavors in it, so it will be more widely accepted, but it still reggae. To be honest, you have to change the sound a little from the ordinary, one-drop, so what's happenin' now, we're puttin' in more instrument, some people mixin' in Indian beat, Indian sounds, but it still reggae.

I think the guys in the studios, they should be takin' more time to create things. I'm not saying all them do it, but most of them gonna wait for something and then make a cover version. It is a waste. You waste lyrics. I'm ready to do three songs on one riddim, but beyond that, it's got to be something really good, for me to go further with it. Unless you have something really good, I'm not gonna do it. If you have "Murder She Wrote" alone, and "Bam Bam," that would be all right, but when you have all the other version, what you think a gonna happen? You cut the sales of that one song. What they should have done is used that lyrics—'cause once the lyrics is written down, you can make a completely different backing. But what most people doin' these days, most people is not confident to do something new. That's a problem. They sit there and they wait, when somebody got a one-hit song, then everybody jump, doin' the same riddim. Personally, it's not good. It's all right, but it's not good.

You don't have a lot of singers nowadays. I don't know what happen. You got DJs endlessly, endless DJs, so at the moment you can probably count all the singers. Frankie Paul, Sanchez, Dennis, Barrington Levy, Freddie, is not many of them. Is more DJs at the moment. There are some good young singers, Norbert Clarke, I done a song with him last weekend, it's a cover version of "Winter World of Love." He sound good. One of my new singers, that's Richie Brown, good voice, you know. There are a lot a them, a lot of good young talent. I have an idea, I'm doin' my main thing, and every other day, I maybe take two or three of them and give them a chance. I say, "Go in there and let me hear how you sound." And if they sound good, I work with them, we do more things. Everybody deserve a chance, and I give every one of them a chance, when I can.

I'm hoping that me get a studio together, because I'm in the studio every day, it cost you money. It best to have your own, because you could be in there every day. Sometime an idea comes up, then you have to start, try to get the time, get your band together, call everybody, and say, "Come over, we have an idea, let's go for it." It's hard, you know. Bobby Digital, his studio is for his work, you can never have his studio. He have his studio and he use it for his stuff alone. Jammy's is the same thing, you know, and those people who get to go in those studios, they are happenin' producers, they are really happenin' at the moment.

I used to do the sound system, I am a selecter, that's where everybody know me from. Stereograph Sound System, it's one of the biggest sounds in Jamaica, and I used to do a combination, Rankin' Joe, and them days, used to put out so much new singers. I used to produce my own sound, because the more exclusive you have . . . these days they call it "special," but I used to call it, those days, "exclusive." I used to produce song with Barry Brown and all them people, and when we played them, we used to say exclusive. I have a long standing as producer from them days, not just the Eighties or Nineties, but from them days.

The Studio One riddims will never die, and the simple reason why Studio One refuse to die is, the next generation comes up, they hear about Studio One, and they gonna love Studio One. The next generation of producer, they're gonna like the Studio One sound. They're gonna say, "I love this sound and I should do something with it in my own style." Studio One is gonna be there, and next generation gonna love Studio One sound. Because everything is original, original song. Studio One and Treasure Isle can never be replaced.

Jah Screw has produced records recently for Barrington Levy, Chaka Demus and Pliers, Admiral Tibet, Richie Brown, and many other reggae artists. He was interviewed at his Kingston home.

SINGER NADINE SUTHERLAND
New York, May 1992

Sister Carol

My position over the years is that the truth have no choice but to come out. Let's put it this way: when things get bad, they get so bad that they hit the bottom, but I believe people will come back up. The whole music, dancehall music, was just getting so slack—people taking off their clothes on stage—it got to that point, where it was getting unbearable to everybody.

I think that a lot of young people in Jamaica figure out that everything is a sellout, the politics is a sellout, the church. So a lot of them turn to music, and the type of music that really helps them in their lives is the conscious type of music. It forces them to look into themselves and see their life and realize that, "Hey, we've been going the wrong way, we need to do something positive." This is really a rewarding feeling for someone like me, 'cause the young DJs are turning in a more positive direction. And the people who want to see it as a bandwagon thing, I would advise them not to, because if you're not going to contribute to it, leave it alone.

I think they should continue to promote what the youth want to talk about. I think they should take it with gratitude. It's the cultural and artistic side of the people. The people who say it's a bandwagon thing, they are jealous, they are the very ones who are guilty. They keep forgetting the example of the biggest person to ever come out of reggae music, and took it international, Bob Marley. There was no compromising. He never had to cross over. The people loved him as he was, the fact that he promoted good things to them. That's what they want.

I try to take the teachings of Marcus Garvey, economic empowerment and things like that, and apply them to what I've been doing. One of the biggest problems, you know, is getting out there to market what you have, and distribute it widely. The new album, we produced it ourselves and went down and gave it to the company for them to release it, you know. The [larger labels] won't really focus the attention on the artist that the artist need, because they've got so many other people that can deliver music of the commercial type. I've never known a record company who have gone out, find young talent, you know, groom them, and prepare them, they never do that. That's the one thing they don't promote, new talent.

I don't see [what I'm doing] as "crossover." No one tells me to do this in order to get mainstream. I've been living in America long enough to know the diversity, the ethnicity, you know, so I've tried to make some tapes that I know that would be appealing to the younger people, a little

SISTER CAROL
"I try to take the teachings of Marcus Garvey and apply them to what I'm doing . . ."
New York, 1994

hip-hop and a little bit of jazz, and things like that, but I've kept the message straight. I did the beats like that because I'm really reachin' out to the youth, you know, but it's not like I did this thing 'cause I want to break through to mainstream. Forget that. My own personal intuition, and my experiences in traveling, have guided me to how I wanted to present this thing. I could record in the roots style, in the original roots style, and the message would be the same.

Hip-hop and rapping kind of sound, all [their] influences are coming from the Jamaican dancehall, you see. You have hip-hop rappers now who are doing hard-core dancehall reggae music, you know, people like KRS-1. They are all drawing on the culture that we have back home [in Jamaica] and they are talking about reality and day-to-day things. You have wars and these things happening, all of these things that you have to reckon with and learn. You have to do something topical, because all of these things that are going on in the ghetto, you have more than enough to think and write about.

Sister Carol was interviewed in fall 1994, shortly after her return from a "spiritually uplifting" trip to Ethiopia. Her current release, called Lyrically Potent, *is available on the Heartbeat label.*

Big Youth

To me, I don't get no inspiration right now, the music, the music is empty, you know what I mean, 'cause it's not an acoustic music, man, with bands—you know what I'm saying? There's no what they call culture, you know. So-called record producers, it's like somebody just pay them to destroy the music, you know what I'm saying? Some people are new to the beat, but I think what they need to do is to listen to the original music, man, try and promote some of that now, and then people will have something to work with, something to develop so that they do something new.

A lot of styles, you notice, they make a song, and after a couple of months, you hear nothin' more. It's like you have dread and dread and what about the real dread, Rasta, is something real. Humanity no love. People need to go and look into themselves and think about family values, that is more culture and reality to me, you understand; what's happening now and what the system doing to you, and that is what you get listening to reggae music. Rock is not Jah music.

BIG YOUTH
"Righteousness exalt a nation . . ."
Kingston, 1994

In my greatest belief today I hear people coming up with consciousness and culture. It's consciousness they need to learn, like them are some true Rastafari, 'cause Rasta is the true conscience of the people. They just come and play with it like a so-called dread joke, when you listen to the great livity of Rasta in the Seventies, you know what I'm saying. Dreadlocks is not Rasta, you know. It don't matter that a man grow dread, it's naturality that is something that is given by the Father.

This is what we need in the music, is togetherness towards the world, towards people, that this mission to deal with people could come about, you know what I'm saying? Today it's disrespect to woman, disrespect to elders, disrespect everybody. What I have to say is that righteousness exalt a nation, you know, and when one has something down there and it's true, man, the truth has got to be heard. I just think that, me, me on the whole, I hold back, just watching the tide, because I couldn't deal with the woman this and the girl that . . . you understand . . . 'cause my way of teaching is about the African daughter, and you cannot disrespect the daughter, and the sister must try and live good and do good, so, everybody must do good.

From the early Nineties, I don't see no great superstar, I don't see nobody make statements, you understand? They need to promote the people that really have something to offer, that could teach a younger one. They should let the message go, let people see what it is, and learn, and be an inspiration instead of trying to drag them down. Talk to me dirty, all this dirty talk, that is nonsense, man. With me, if I say something that I know makes sense, even if only ten people get the record, at least you try to save ten people, convert ten people to consciousness. This music is not all about money, this music is about humanity, it's our media, that's where we teach.

If the media was trying to help, which the media should be teachers also, that's what they are there for. In our days, you know, we were trying to tell the truth, no crap, you know. You tell the truth, to be conscious, to get up off the ground 'cause you're down there for too long. Think conscious, check for your brother. Well, if people really checking for each other, living good, then all these wars and crime wouldn't go on, but it seems like some part of the system want that, so they just use the media to trick up the people's mind.

Big Youth, one of the first reggae artists to bring Rasta consciousness to the dance hall, is still going strong after more than twenty years in the music business. He is still touring and recently released albums in France and Jamaica.

IJAHMAN LEVI
New York, 1995

J. C. Lodge

At the moment I'm not totally happy with the direction that we're heading in, because reggae right now is being, I think, flooded by the DJ thing. Though there is a place for a DJ and I don't have anything against DJ, because I think it's a valid part of reggae, it's just I think that the whole thing is just overbalanced right now in that direction. In some ways it is doing something for reggae, because in America, for example, it's taken a number of years for reggae to break into certain areas, and it is happening now through the dancehall style of reggae, because there's a link between dancehall reggae and rap music in America, and the youths on both sides, in America and here, have a lot in common. They have similar views and the way they dress, the attitude is very similar, you know. So there is that common link there and that's what's helping it to spread in America. That's a step for reggae there, it's becoming exposed to people that it wasn't before. But, on the other hand, I want to see more of a balance.

Singers, like myself, in reggae, I think I speak on behalf of them when I say that I hope that a lot of these major companies now that are signing up the DJs will also be aware that there are other facets to reggae and not just project reggae at that. You know, money is always the name of the game, and this is a trend now because one or two DJs have created this big stir overseas, all of a sudden all the companies seem to be, like vultures, or John Crow, as we say here, circling and trying to decide who's the next DJ and signin' everybody, you know. It's a little bit hurtful to people who have been in the business for years and tried to maintain a certain standard, and struggled for the sake of the standard, to see people coming out overnight and becoming a huge success, all this excitement around them, being signed up and all that.

I'm curious to see what's going to happen, because another thing that I find about the dancehall thing, it's a culturally ethnic thing, I mean the language that's spoken and everything. I'm curious to see what's going to happen when these people have all this money behind them, and they're pushed up there, and they have these fantastic videos, and they pull up in limos, they're bedecked in gold chains and flashy clothes, and I wonder, what's going to happen after that? I'm dying to see what's going to happen, and see maybe if my whole value system is wrong or something.

J. C. LODGE
"All over the world, in really strange places, people are attracted to reggae . . ."
New Kingston

A sad thing that I find is that, in Jamaica, a lot of people be-come known and become popularized because they do fifty songs a week for different producers, and because they have so much mate-rial they can't help but be heard and noticed. Which I think will eventually turn against them, when they have a deal, because they'll find that their better stuff is probably gone already. But also, when they are signed now, you have all these little smaller companies com-ing out with stuff, and the bigger companies spent all this money launching a particular record, and then they come out. The buying public, they don't care, they'll buy anything, as long as it's this guy. Artists like myself now, who have been careful over the years—times have been hard for me, like a lot of people, you have times when you're not making any money—and it would be very easy to go check a producer, and say, "Do a tune with me and get in a dance," and do that several times, which is what these people do. But I made the sacrifice not to do that because I was trying to have a proper ca-reer.

The other problem that I have found is that . . . I do reggae, I mean that's my main thing, but I don't do only reggae, so this album, *Tropic of Love*, has a mixture of stuff on it, and I find in America, the problem is been, they don't know how to market it because I'm not one thing. I do a bit of rapping, deejaying, I sing, I do non-reggae stuff, so they just don't know how to market me. I don't think that is a problem for me anywhere else except America, everything has to be in a category because the charts are all different. Even like "Tele-phone Love," which has been my biggest hit in America, some peo-ple call it a dancehall tune, some say lovers' rock. The beat is a dancehall beat, you could deejay on it fine.

The thing is, I don't ever want to give up on reggae, but I find that doing reggae makes it even harder to be "happening." I can't avoid the fact that if I just did some ballads and some dance, disco-type stuff, I'm sure I'd have gotten much further ahead than this, es-pecially in America. People say to me, in Jamaica now, "Why do you keep bothering with reggae, you know, you can do something else." But I guess it's in me, so I don't want to give up on it. One of the reasons that I haven't given up on reggae, apart from the fact that I love it, is that all over the world, really strange places, people are attracted to it. It makes me wonder why, what do they like about reggae?

Being a woman performer, I'm one of a really, really, small mi-nority, and I long for the day when I feel that I have been taken a bit

BUJU BANTON
Reggae Sunsplash, 1992

STUDIO TECHNOLOGY — NEW STYLE
Producer Noel Browne at New Name Studio, Kingston

more seriously by my peers, my male peers. I've met musicians who've said, "Boy, you sing wicked" or "You had a wicked song the other day," and so on, but I find that, when I get down to work with them—and at the moment I have not got my own band, so I work with a lot of different people all the time, every time I have a show it's a different set of people—I find in a lot of cases I'm not taken as serious as I'd like to be taken. Like if I request something to be played a particular way, I get a sort of vibe like, "What do you know?" But that's all part of the growing, that's something that we all have to go through, not just me, everybody who doesn't have their own band, that's what we have to go through, although for women it's a little bit harder. And I think there is a lack of respect for women in general in Jamaica, a lot of that.

The world in general, the whole value system has gone down, and unfortunately I'm one of these negative people who think things are only going to get worse. I don't think it's going to get any better.

STUDIO TECHNOLOGY — OLD STYLE
Jah D's Food, Clothes and Shelter Studio, Kingston

Generally speaking, values have fallen, and people are all into having the best car, the best house, the best clothes. I observe that, sometimes I laugh in what I hear, but what makes me not laugh is when I see people taken in by it, and disregarding other forms that are more worthwhile, or moral. In Jamaica, because of our whole economical conditions, you find that a lot of youths are getting into the music business who perhaps could have done something else, but because they think it's something where they can instantly make the big bucks, they go into it. And everybody can't be a musician—there's got to be some audience. You can't have a show where everybody is on stage. So it's amusing, but in a way it's sad, too.

Singer-songwriter J. C. Lodge's latest album, Love for All Seasons, *is on RAS Records. She was interviewed at her home in New Kingston.*

GUSSIE CLARKE
"Technology is making some people lazy . . ."
Anchor Recording, Kingston, 1992

Gussie Clarke

I believe that the changes in the business recently are due to the mentality and the intent of the new producers and artists. They are more business oriented, where in the past it was more personal, you know, competition between Duke Reid and Treasure Isle, the various producers. People right now is thinking business and trying to correct some of the mistakes that happened in the past.

From what I have seen, DJs seem to have a higher ego than singers, and you know, each one try to outdo the other, in recording, who have the most gold, who have the most cars, to be the guy on top, which is a short-term view of the reality of the recording industry. Some producers might think in this whole short-term mentality, like, "OK, this riddim is happening, it's great, let's exploit it, let's make money." Producers who lack a certain level of creativity will re-record this riddim and use it so many times and try to cash in. It's not the way to go, if you look at it from an industry point of view, and we would like to be respected as any other industry that exist in the world. It is not the way to go, but many don't see it.

Taking an older riddim, I can understand that, one is revitalizing or refreshing it, as long as them get the whole copyright thing together, but many of them lack the knowledge of the infringements that they have committed, and it's going to be a hell of a problem at some point in time. I think that the only copyright law that can come to this country, or the one way it can work, the money that is being paid for mechanical royalties must be paid at the point where the record is being manufactured. 'Cause I mean, many people a do business out of them car or them shop or them house, so there's no way that one would be able to collect mechanical royalties due to original artist and composers, and some of them will even play ignorant so as not to pay. Let us set up our own ASCAP in Jamaica, or BMI, or something equal to that, then the money can be channeled. A little man who just was a gunman and tomorrow he's a record producer, only way you're going to get him pay, you're going to have to shoot him, too. So the only way it can be done is at the point of manufacturing.

The business might be better, but the technology is allowing us to make it so simple and so easy that the whole way of learning and doing things, and that commitment, don't exist anymore, that urge to learn and that urge to create. The technology is making some people lazy. Musicians now turn up in studio two hours late. I mean,

MYSTIC REVEALERS
Reggae Sunsplash, 1993

when a producer is paying like 300, 400 dollars per hour, a guy turns up two hours late, he has lost 800 dollars, and to him it's no big thing, you know. We need to tighten up all of that.

And trying to fuse too much of that hip-hop or funk or whatever that kind of music, one has to be very careful of trying to lose yours to catch on to something else—we have to be very careful there. The irony is that many people, to my knowledge, trying to fuse with reggae, and reggae people here is trying to fuse to their thing, so let's hope we don't get lost somewhere in the middle. You hear reggae in the States, jeans ads, many things, movies, and alla that, people are catching on. So we should tighten up the business part and go deeper in the whole creativity to capitalize, you know, before everybody come in and want to take it. Then you have nothing, you know. But many of us think that way, fast bucks, and we have a problem.

I don't think technology will allow us to go back to where we were. Where we were is an era that we have left but will remain in our minds, and people will always go back to it for specific reasons, not generally. The little kid who is in high school right now is going to play everything off a computer and a keyboard. What interest does he have in going back in the whole analog situation? Life has made it easy. You just have to play one bar and loop it and you have a song. It will not go back. It is the age of computers. We here, we will not be the next generation of people who going to be doing this thing. The next generation will be our kids, and they are going to take the simplest way. Digital technology and computers are more accurate than humans, and it offers them levels of creativity that we didn't have coming up. One can make so many changes, it is a lot of brain work to really accurately program a song in a computer and get it as how you'd want it. The human feel, that's the part we're going to lose, but then smart kids going to come and find their way around it.

Live musicians will always be around, though. People love to go and hear a band play, people love that level of entertainment. There's no fun, you know man, just playing tracks and an artist singing. The fun will have gone out of that. Musicians will always be around. And the ones who will learn in the old ways will be unique, because everybody going to the shortcuts. So it will be unique to know the old way and be able to play the old way and also use this newer technology. So a guy who try to learn at that level will be a musician in demand.

Veteran producer Augustus "Gussie" Clarke owns Anchor Recording, one of Jamacia's premier studios in Kingston, where he was interviewed.

PRESSING RECORDS AT TUFF GONG

Coxsone Dodd

Recycling of original riddims keep the original alive, and you can really hear the difference between imitation and real sounds. And it's not hurtin', it's really helpin' keep the original alive, though I think, as an original musician, I think it's really killing the musician, it's discouraging the good musician. Non-employment because of the computer and whatever it is. What they're actually doing is sampling and looping and programming, and these are done by non-musicians, right? So I don't think too much of it. There is a need for restructuring the whole thing, because as it is going now and the musician are being discouraged, then you have got nobody who is going through musical training anymore. Everybody is just going with the vibes, like, they feel that this would run nice here, they feel like that there, that's it. The truth is that it hasn't got a sound of its own—all the music sound alike.

Now, what do I think of the Jamaican Copyright Act? Well, that's a must, and I think it's the best thing that ever happened for Jamaica since independence, and now that it's a law, I think that every creative person will benefit. It's gonna take some time, but what I figure if you are sampling and using another person idea, then you've got to pay for the use of the product. So far I've been in contact with quite a few of the producer, which I will call the reducers, because they are willing, because it's obvious in any court they couldn't stand up, because some of the song, they run it from the record straight onto their tape and just dub little things around it, anybody can do it, there is no creativity there.

And when it comes to the DJ who seem to be so much in the forefront today, they won't change the direction of the future of reggae. They don't spend enough time puttin' the lyrics together and dealin' with sensible topics with a day-to-day cultural lyrics. What I figure in the earlier days, it really was a love and devotion for the music, so we were more cautious of the kind of lyrics. [Nowadays] they don't care what sort of rubbish they feed to the kids, you understand, which is bad influence. And as far as the DJ with the gun and violence, it really have a influence on the youth. Because whatever is popular, like, you have a gun for me, the kids going to school and singing that, and they are living it too, because everybody has a gun on them, so this is why you find the gun in the school. So I don't think too much of the toasting and boasting and the ignorance they

CLEMENT "SIR COXSONE" DODD
"In the earlier days, it really was a love and devotion for the music . . ."
New York, 1994

are putting today [into] the songs. Because some of the done-over riddims, they're not bad, but what they got to offer? You understand?

One little thing that I would like to really get over is that there has been a album that is *Birth of a Legend* [1977] by Bob Marley and the Wailers, which has been released by Columbia for over fifteen years. And I've tried very hard to collect even a cent and haven't been able to collect even a penny from Columbia, and you see today I am looking around and seen a lot of the Wailers product coming from all over. I've never licensed these to other people. But I figure more or less, company like Columbia, they realize they did a deal with somebody, and these people are out of the business, these are gangsters and whatever it is, and they know the product belongs to me, so why not make some kind of settlement? . . . I'm not expectin' that they're going to give me the right count, but havin' a thing for fifteen years . . . but we have been in touch with them, but for about ten years they have been sending me to the people who they say they license it from, and then we realize these people are out of the business, because the government had found them in some racketeering business. But it's clear in the liner notes that Clement Dodd recorded these songs and was the first Bob Marley and the Wailers tracks. I'm not lying!

It would be nice if the readers realize that the earlier producers really been through a lot, and this was being used to get even the Wailers from me, because, after this guy come to me and ask about certain royalties, and I can't present them with a statement. What I had to be doing as a gentleman, was, here's an advance, an advance from royalty until I get a statement, and I never did get a statement even up to now, so, even now that Bunny Wailer, who at one time was so difficult, he's so close to me when he came to realize that all these time, and even, Chris [Blackwell] told them that I had been collecting royalty and whatever, put the guys against me, and they went with them [Island]. And now that the whole thing has boiled down, now they realize what went down.

Clement "Coxsone" Dodd, a true pioneer of reggae, has produced more than 200 albums and thousands of singles on the Studio One label. He was interviewed at his record store and studio, Music City, in Brooklyn, New York.

ORIGINAL SKATALITE JOHNNY "DIZZY" MOORE
Kingston, 1995

ORIGINAL SKATALITES ROLAND ALPHONSO AND THE LATE TOMMY McCOOK
New York, 1995

THIRD WORLD
"Nobody is scared of Rasta any more . . ."
West Kingston, April 1992

Third World

BUNNY RUGS: I don't think we'll ever have another Bob Marley situation. But he did such fantastic work. Third World have been out there for a long time, and Third World was one of the first set of Jamaican musicians who were brave enough to try something of a difference. We have been ridiculed for it over the years, but eventually it just started to pay off now. I like the new direction of music. But I'm a little bit disappointed in black music, in the fact that I can't tell who is who now. Everything is MIDI and samples and stuff.

Dreadlocks is now a trend, where you can shave one side of your head, and one side is dread and the other is completely bald. What they have done is taken certain elements out of the culture, out of reggae culture, the dread, particular rhythms. Jamaican music, reggae music, it was raw instruments, drums, bass, keyboards, and the dub music keep putting in and taking out instruments and phrasing and stuff. That part of it have influenced American music now. Hip-hop—instruments keep flying in and out. But the actual *message* of what reggae was saying, and what Bob was saying, and Peter Tosh, people like that, I don't think they have paid *any* attention to that at all. And that is why I am disappointed. I don't hear any message.

There's so many black musicians, so many talented drummers, talented bass players, talented keyboard players, why we can't hear them? Why we hear just one guy doin' everything? I hate when I take up an album and look at it, one guy sing and write all the songs and produce all the tracks. After a while, it becomes boring.

First time when you heard Donny Hathaway, when you heard Marvin Gaye, when you heard Stevie Wonder, they are individuals, their music is individualized. When you hear James Brown, you know right away who that is. Nowadays you can't tell, unless the disc jockey on the radio say, "That was Sam Soft, man," you don't know who it was. I think the public in general is getting really wary. That's why records no sell. Apart from the economy and stuff, but people always buy records—they wait for their favorite artist to come out with the stuff and they go out and buy it.

The reason why old songs will always sound fresh is those days you designed a song, you put it together so it will last, like cars, is you buy certain cars and you know you can have them for ten, fifteen years, and they'll still function, they'll still perform. Nowadays, songs, we hear them two weeks, three weeks, you don't want to hear them again. That is why we have to get back to songs that have meaning. You don't have to be political, you don't have to be violent, you don't have to tell everybody to praise God, just good music.

RICHIE DALEY: The audience is different now, because all those who were babies, who were born when it just hit the world and the U.S.A., these people are now adults, and they grew up on reggae. They grew up on Bob Marley, Third World, Toots, and the Maytals, and to them there are no barriers, in terms of, they don't see it as something quite as alienating as the older audience, which we introduced it to at that time. They are much more open-minded to it, you know. A lot of the kids, a lot of people today who are executives in recording companies, we remember playing for them in high schools and colleges. And now they are like the directors and they are like directin' videos and they are like A&R people in the recording company, so their whole perspective is totally different, so it show great promise in that sense.

Before, we couldn't get this music played on main station radio. People were still viewing it as something very ethnic, and slotted it, and it had like all kinda connotations tied up with it. And now you got a club in New York, and a club just about anywhere, and they're hoppin' to this music, it's just another song to them. The hip-hop and the reggae are mixin' together, not crossin' over. There was a word in our time, early time, when they talk about crossover; there is no such thing as a crossover anymore. When you used the word crossover, it was keepin' one point and crossin' over to another point; now, the whole thing is one, so there is no crossin' over, it's just there. There is nowhere to cross over to anymore.

I think reggae take its place in the world now. We have always known that it was a true music that couldn't be suppressed by anyone. And I am fortunate enough to have lived to see that. I knew Bob Marley when he was a virtually unknown entity, until he is now one massive cult figure, even after he passed away in the physical sense. So many years, and his music still live on. There has to be something really deep there. It is limitless.

WILLIE STEWART: Reggae into the Nineties is gonna be big. I think going to be huge. Shabba Ranks, Maxi Priest, breakthrough artists, I think a lot more people are used to the whole changes, the

THIRD WORLD
(*left to right*) Rugs, Cat, Ibo, Richie, Willie
Video shoot, Kingston

lyrics, they like it, Jamaica, with the hotel industry, all the people can expose Jamaica, because tourists come and they ask for reggae. It's just a matter of time now. There are a lot of artists comin' forward and presentin' themself with good packages—good lyrics, good show—and the world come to hear.

I think it was very hard to crack the market, to get any airplay was very hard in our time. On the road, we played with people like Country Joe and the Fish, people like Santana. It was very hard, people never hear where you breaking new ground. And today, when you talk about reggae music, people know Bob, they know Jamaica, they know about it. The work has paid off, the communication. People tell us here in Jamaica, they say "Bob Marley" first before they say "Kingston" or "Jamaica." So it has paid off. Over the years it was very hard, but it has paid off for people like Shabba Ranks. The road has been made, and all the new artists who go up there, the sky is the limit.

CAT COORE: Reggae is moving along the road. I think we're moving along, and it's building on its previous achievements. Reggae music is not like one of these musics that go up big for, like, two years. Everybody listen to disco music, you know, and then it's gone. From the Seventies it's been growing, growing, growing, little, little,

little, and it's always, every time it move, it stays there and it moves higher. The music is on a nice little high now. It's just to get back people into good songs, you know. Everybody's off into DJ now, it's just fun time, DJ is just one of those musics that is for fun.

Japan and certain countries in the Far East are just picking up onto reggae now, like how the States was in the Seventies. There was a big boom for it in the Seventies, California, all over the States, but it is more accepted now. But that boom is going on now in Japan and those places. So you have to think of it in that way, you have to kind of realize that this is a new thing.

IBO COOPER: From my perspective and probably all of Third World, we have seen a war won, a dream come true, in that when we came out to the United States first, 1976, there was still a lot of people, if not the majority of people, who did not know what reggae was, had not heard the music. It was a new phenomenon for everybody in the United States, irrespective of race, class, color, or creed. We were therefore one of the pioneers, along with Jimmy Cliff, Bob Marley, Peter Tosh, Toots, some of the early people, yeah? We came out there and in many territories we were the first reggae band they'd ever heard—live, they probably had heard records and tapes—but I remember definitely we played the Pipeline in Seattle,

and it was the first time that reggae had played live in Seattle. We had a large turnout of American people and they loved it.

In those days there were a lot of people who were skeptical of [reggae's] moneymaking possibilities, skeptical, of its being popular across the whole nation, they were skeptical, but we kept on going. Come the Eighties, we saw record companies looking at it closer, looking at the culture closer, and trying to understand what the people were about and what the whole thing was about. And then coming down to the late Eighties and early Nineties, we finally saw not only the Grammy awards looking at a reggae category, but we actually saw platinum-selling artists in UB40, Ziggy Marley, Shabba Ranks, Maxi Priest went number one on the pop charts. So in a way we have made an impact.

Unfortunately, though, the out-and-out roots-and-culture music is fading now in the eyes of a more commercial cross-culture music of reggae and rap and R&B and rock. More of the rap and R&B reggae is popular now, say, even than rock reggae, which was an early experiment. I say unfortunately, because it has more of a blatant commercial overtone. Everybody's looking for the next charts and the next Grammy rather than a certain meaning and feeling that was there in the more Rasta-rock era.

I know the world has changed. I know we have won some of the wars. The Berlin Wall came down, apartheid is fading, the world is becoming more of a human place, which is some of the things we were trying to achieve. So we can't go on fighting the old revolutions if they are over. I agree with that. However, if some things happening that seem to be turning the thing back a ways, you might now be giving in to a certain permissiveness in terms of, say, drugs, or crime, which is not what we want to achieve. We want to achieve happiness, yes, we wanted to party, we did want to have a good time, but there have got to be some guidelines about a good time, you know? And that's just my worry. It's a little too raw sometimes, for my tastes. But we got the acceptance, we got the world to turn around, we got people to look seriously at the environment, racism, oppression, and we have won some revolutions. I am satisfied with those changes, political impact on Jamaica and so on. Nobody is scared of Rasta anymore; it's accepted; it's something that people look at with more seriousness now. Those things have been won.

"Reggae ambassadors" Third World were interviewed while taping a video for their 1992 album, Committed.

DANCEHALL STYLE AND FASHION
Reggae Sunfest, Montego Bay

JAMAICA'S FINEST

Acknowledgements

I am very pleased to see the release of the U.S. version of *Reggae Island*. It has been an incredible experience putting this project together. Having been a reggae fan for more than half my life, my love for Jamaica and reggae has brought me many interesting experiences, this being one of them. Getting to meet, hang out with, and hear stories from your favorite singers and musicians is something I feel extremely lucky to have been able to do. Reggae music is something that really has to be experienced in order to get the full effect of it: the sights, sounds, smells, and vibrations, all in one place, Jamaica.

In doing this book I have made many good friends and also seen the loss of quite a few. But it has taught me many things along the way. The one problem with a book like this is that you can't include everybody, not to mention trying to find everyone. I still wish I could have reached those crucial few I have been trying to track down. Maybe next time.

There are too many people who helped out to possibly mention, but I do have to thank the following: the God who makes all things possible . . . Mom and Dad . . . Sharon Burke and June Heslop of the Solid Agency for their help . . . Chinna and the High Times Ltd. crew, can't thank you enough . . . Yvette at Sandosa Music . . . all the people at Specs/Shang . . . Henry K . . . Harris . . . SLM for your assistance . . . and an extra special big-up to Tex and the New Kingston crew for all your special services . . . nuff respect! . . . and most of all to the artists who contributed their words, thoughts, ideas, and insight, maximum respect and honor . . . Jah guide.

BRIAN JAHN

Years before I ever set foot on Jamaican soil, I was introduced to this beautiful and complex society through the works of its writers. Respect is due to Roger Mais, Peter Abrahams, Perry Henzell, Michael Thelwell, Orlando Patterson, V. C. Reid, Charles Hyatt, Louise Bennett, Christine Craig, Patricia Powell, and Anthony Winkler; also to non-Jamaicans Russell Banks and Zora Neale Hurston.

Guidance was provided by earlier works on reggae music by Garth White, Dermot Hussey, Timothy White, Michael Thomas, Stephen Davis, Peter Simon, Billy Bergman, Jeremy Marre, Hannah Charlton, Sebastian Clarke, and Dick Hebdige, which helped expose music lovers around the world to the diversity of Jamaican culture.

Studies of world musics and cultures by Charles Keil, Stephen Feld, Renato Rosaldo, Jocelyne Guilbault, Peter Manuel, and James Lull provided the theoretical basis for the text, as did more general works by Gordon K. Lewis, Paolo Freire, Walter Rodney, and Frantz Fanon.

Several academic colleagues willingly lent their insights to this project: Carolyn Cooper of the University of the West Indies, Mona; Ewart Skinner, Peter Shields, Nancy Brendlinger, and Steven Cornelius of Bowling Green State University; Bill Doan of Gannon University; and Anita Waters of Denison University.

Special thanks to Joseph Hill, for a conversation on a tour bus in Cleveland that helped shape this book; to the Ark Band of Columbus, Ohio; and to Errol Lam, Howard Campbell, Annie Paul, Andrea Davis, Lloyd Stanbury, Roger Steffens, Winston Grennan, Nancy Lewis, Papa Pilgrim, Tom Pearson, Reggae Ambassadors Worldwide, all posse, and crew everywhere.

TOM WEBER

Index of Interviews

Other titles of interest

AFRICA O-YE!
A Celebration of African Music
Graeme Ewens
215 pp., over 200 photos, maps and
illus., 110 in color
80461-1 $27.95

ARE YOU EXPERIENCED?
The Inside Story of the
Jimi Hendrix Experience
Noel Redding and Carol Appleby
258 pp., 28 photos
80681-9 $14.95

ASCENSION
John Coltrane and His Quest
Eric Nisenson
298 pp.
80644-4 $13.95

BLACK MUSIC
LeRoi Jones (Amiri Imamu Baraka)
288 pp., 4 photos
80814-5 $14.95

BLACK TALK
Ben Sidran
228 pp., 16 photos
80184-1 $10.95

THE BOOKS OF AMERICAN
NEGRO SPIRITUALS
Two volumes in one
James Weldon & J.R. Johnson
384 pp.
80074-8 $15.95

BROTHER RAY
Ray Charles' Own Story
Updated Edition
Ray Charles and David Ritz
370 pp., 30 photos
80482-4 $14.95

BROWN SUGAR
Eighty Years of America's
Black Female Superstars
Donald Bogle
208 pp., 183 photos
80380-1 $17.95

CHASIN' THE TRANE
The Music and Mystique of
John Coltrane
J. C. Thomas
256 pp., 16 pp. of photos
80043-8 $12.95

THE DA CAPO GUIDE
TO CONTEMPORARY
AFRICAN MUSIC
Ronnie Graham
316 pp., 16 pp. of photos
80325-9 $13.95

DIVIDED SOUL
The Life of Marvin Gaye
David Ritz
367 pp., 47 photos
80443-3 $13.95

THE HENDRIX
EXPERIENCE
Mitch Mitchell and John Platt
176 pp., 201 illus.
(including 71 in color)
80818-8 $24.95

I PUT A SPELL ON YOU
The Autobiography of Nina Simone
with Stephen Cleary
207 pp., 28 photos
80525-1 $13.95

I'D RATHER BE THE DEVIL
Skip James and the Blues
Stephen Calt
400 pp., 13 pp. of illus.
80579-0 $14.95

JOHN COLTRANE
Bill Cole
278 pp., 25 photos
80530-8 $14.95

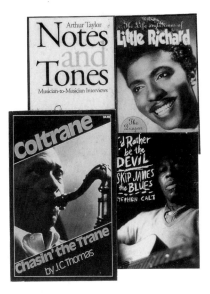